Celebrating

the Rest

of Your Life

A Baby Boomer's Guide to Spirituality

David Yount

Augsburg Books
MINNEAPOLIS

For Becky

Grow old along with me!
The best is yet to be.
—Robert Browning

To see a World in a Grain of Sand
And a Heaven in a Wild Flower
Hold Infinity in the palm of your hand
And Eternity in an Hour.
—William Blakey

CELEBRATING THE REST OF YOUR LIFE
A Baby Boomer's Guide to Spirituality

Copyright © 2005 by David Yount. All rights reserved. Except for brief quotations in critical articles or reviews, no part of this book may be reproduced without prior written permission from the publisher. Write to: Permissions, Augsburg Fortress, Publishers, P.O. Box 1209, Minneapolis, MN 55440-1209.

Large-quantity purchases or custom editions of this book are available at a discount from the publisher. For more information, contact the sales department at Augsburg Fortress, Publishers, P.O. Box 1209, Minneapolis, MN 55440-1209.

Scripture passages are from the Holy Bible, New International Version®, copyright © 1973, 1978, 1984 International Bible Society. Used by permission of Zondervan Publishing House. All rights reserved.

Cover design by Laurie Ingram; cover photo © Jim Richardson/CORBIS
Book design by Michelle L. N. Cook

ISBN 0-8066-5171-7

The paper used in this publication meets the minimum requirements of American National Standard for Information Sciences—Permanence of Paper for Printed Library Materials, ANSI Z329.48-1985. ∞™

Manufactured in the U.S.A.

09   08   07   06   05   1   2   3   4   5   6   7   8   9   10

Table of Contents

Preface:

Making Vows

The young Henry David Thoreau, urged by friends to prepare his soul for the next life, complained, "One world at a time!"[1] Thoreau died prematurely at the age of forty-five, still in his prime. Had he lived longer, I suspect he would have reconsidered his cavalier dismissal of eternity. At the very least, that most reflective of Americans might have pondered how to spend the rest of his life.

Every eight seconds an American man or woman reaches the age of fifty.[2] If you are a baby boomer, you may be approaching your later years in the company of seventy-seven million other Americans born during the years following World War II.[3] You escaped the Great Depression that humbled your parents and the Second World War. Perhaps the death of a parent or a friend or your own serious illness has given you intimations of your own mortality. Every year since I was a small child, I have been reminded on Ash Wednesday that I came from dust and to dust will return. Now I take the reminder more seriously. Having lived already half a century, it is time for you to reflect on life, to savor it, and to plan ahead.

On average, men reaching fifty today can look forward to 27.5 more years of life. A fifty-year-old woman today can anticipate 31.6 more years.[4] But what will ensure the quality of life in our remaining years, and what will strengthen our confidence in a future beyond this life?

Books written for people in middle age tend to cluster around three themes: extending one's life span, planning financially for retirement, and preparing for decline and death. The first books are predictably upbeat, the second are practical, and the third are philosophical.

Unfortunately, no one has yet devised a foolproof recipe for a long and healthy life. Perhaps one day our bodies will be overhauled by genetic engineering and our lives extended. If so, it will be too late for me, born in 1934. At the moment I can depend only on the genes I inherited from my parents, who lived into their eighties but lingered in less than robust health. Their later years were not golden. They only survived retirement, lacking the resources—mental, physical, and financial—to enjoy it. Although both of them were religious, my parents did not meet their final days with equanimity. With forethought, you and I can do better.

Typically, men and women are advised to become more philosophical as they grow older. That is not my counsel. Being philosophical can sometimes mean being resigned to fate, reducing one's expectations, and concentrating on security rather than enjoyment. Of course, everyone experiences good and ill fortune during the course of their lives, but our destinies are not writ in the stars. Accidents and coincidences unpredictably help or hinder us, but only we can plot our lives and decide what to pursue, be it pleasure or accomplishment.

We are, if not quite masters of our fate, yet rich in hope, because we are God's own creatures, made in God's image to enjoy God's company eternally. So, instead of being philosophical in the autumn of our earthly lives, we do better to become theological—to see ourselves from our Designer's perspective. Our bodies inevitably age, but our souls are immune from the ravages of time. Our spirits are forever young. We are never too old to grow young in spirit.

In our mature years, theology is eminently practical. When G. K. Chesterton each summer sought out vacation lodgings for his family, he did not inquire of his prospective landlady how often she changed her guests' sheets or how well she fed her lodgers. Such an inquiry, he sensed, would be impolite.

Instead, Chesterton inquired of his prospective hostess, "What is your theology of the universe?" The puckish pundit reasoned that if the landlady believed in an orderly universe filled with hope, and trusted a generous God to love God's creatures and treat them equitably, she would most likely provide clean bed linen and satisfying meals to her guests.[5]

The Creator who made us in God's likeness never ages; God is forever young. Calling on God's grace, we can *grow* young even as our days dwindle down, and we can find a richness in life that eluded us in our youth. A wise bishop once noted that God has much more in mind than religion. Because God is the author of all that exists, life itself and its fullness are the Creator's preoccupation.

Living—not piety—is the subject of these pages. If your todays and tomorrows are only repetitions of your yesterdays, you are not living as well as you might. As you age, your life should expand, not contract, and your spirit should grow.

Retirement is a gift baby boomers work and save for, an opportunity to do what they always wanted but lacked the leisure for. But retirement is badly named: it is not a retreat from life but only from a nine-to-five existence toiling on someone else's agenda. What you will want to do as you approach retirement is to set your own agenda. It may prove to be busier and more demanding than your workaday life, but it will be more rewarding precisely because it will be your investment in yourself. Think of retirement as your renaissance.

But woe to the man or woman who looks forward to doing nothing in retirement! I have known successful people who, on retiring, lost all sense of self-worth and enjoyment and could not bring themselves even to change their clothes each morning. In his late nineties, comedian George Burns confessed that the hardest task he faced every day was getting his old bones out of bed, but once up he became a dynamo, the perfect picture of a man with humor, a zest for enjoyment, and gratitude for being alive.

Christians who pray for "eternal rest," I suspect, have never really lived. As a child, I was taught that this world is a "vale of tears," to be stoically endured until happily exchanged for eternal bliss. To be sure, too many lives are vales of tears. In the Third World, for example, twenty-four thousand men, women, and children die each day from starvation alone.[6] They have good reason to think of death as deliverance. You and I do not. We must plan for living.

Not long ago, I wrote a book on the subject of the afterlife.[7] Actually, it was about living every day in the light of eternity. Heaven is not a retirement village. In eternity we will not trade in tired old personalities for something better. Rather, we will be the identical persons in eternity, somehow glorified and purified, but the same nonetheless. So what we make of ourselves this side of paradise is what will determine the eternities we enjoy. If we lack a sense of humor now, we can't expect to acquire one in heaven. If we fail to smell the roses in our own gardens now, there will be no flowers gracing our paradise.

When you reach an age when retirement is in sight, it will be time to begin cultivating enjoyment, stretching your mind, expanding your spirit, dropping your emotional guard, and investing in others less fortunate than you. It will be time to trade in mere acquaintanceship for true friendship, and to cultivate community beyond those who live within your domestic walls.

Unfortunately, many looking ahead to retirement are ill-prepared financially, mentally, and spiritually for later life. Only a minority grasp what they are living for as they confront the final decades of their lives on earth. Nearly half of all Americans spend more than they earn. The rest, on average, set aside only a nickel of every dollar they earn for their so-called golden years. Fewer than a third have either a pension or long-term savings to sustain them through retirement. Only 15 percent can expect to be assisted by their families; all fear declining health.[8]

Although the vast majority of those who are approaching their later years profess a belief in God, many are spiritually destitute. Whereas half of today's elderly are regular churchgoers, seven out of ten baby boomers have been sleeping in on Sundays for years. As a consequence, they lack the spiritual resources to confront the rest of their lives with hope and equanimity, let alone with relish.

Lord Byron relished life, all the more because he knew that life's days were limited and weighed down with routine. "When one subtracts from life infancy (which is vegetation), sleep, eating and swilling, buttoning and unbuttoning—how much remains of downright existence?" the poet demanded. His reply: "The summer of a dormouse!"[9]

Time compresses as one progresses through life, becoming more precious with every new year. Simone de Beauvoir sighed: "One day I said to myself, 'I'm forty!' By the time I recovered from the shock of that discovery I had reached fifty." Playwright Christopher Fry, now in his nineties, confesses that he seems to be having breakfast every five minutes. Writer John Mortimer, in his late eighties, cautions, "The aging process is not gradual or gentle. It rushes up, pushes you over, and runs off laughing." He concludes, with good humor: "No one should grow old who isn't ready to appear ridiculous."[10]

Mortimer keeps busy. He has written or edited more than three dozen books, plus film and television scripts, but confesses that "old age entails a good deal of sitting and staring into space"—something I saw a lot of when my parents lingered in nursing homes during the last decades of their lives.

Still, only 5 percent of older Americans are currently consigned to nursing homes.[11] The rest are on their own, still vital, still growing, still enjoying . . . and still complaining. "What a drag it is getting old," Mick Jagger and Keith Richards protest, and their faces show it. Yet the Stones roll on. Television news anchor Tom Brokaw bewailed the day he turned fifty: "It's not that I'm angry or melancholy. It's more an irritation. Sort of a chronic low-level virus." Brokaw believes aging is an invitation: "It's time to be a real grown-up." But he laments: "If I still wore mittens, I'd still lose them."[12]

True maturity is less elusive than Brokaw admits. When Jimmy Carter turned seventy, Barbara Walters asked him, "What have been your best years?" The former president answered honestly, "*Now* is the best time of all."[13] Incidentally, contrary to suspicion, younger Americans respect their elders: about 82 percent suspect seniors have higher moral values, and 75 percent even believe wisdom comes with age.[14]

The writer of Ecclesiastes acknowledged "There is a time for everything, and a season for every activity under heaven" (3:1). There are insects that are born in the morning, become sexually mature in the afternoon, and are dead by nightfall. In the past, human life itself was brief. In ancient Greece the average life span was thirty-eight. In Rome it was only twenty-five, and thirty during the Dark Ages. Those Americans born on the very first Fourth of July could expect to live, on average, only to thirty-five.[15]

Today, by contrast, when we approach retirement we still have a lot of living to look forward to. I like to think that life is like high school or college, and that those of us who have contemplated retirement are in the senior class, lots smarter than we once were, and more capable. Those of us who are spiritually alive relish the opportunity to exit the rat race, simplify down to basic satisfactions, and anticipate our eventual demise serenely as our ticket to eternity. By this measure, death is graduation and commencement.

The great actress Helen Hayes was in her final years when my wife and I were privileged to play host to her at the National Press Club. After greeting members of the Washington press corps, Miss Hayes was clearly exhausted. Yet, when she came to the microphone to introduce her late husband's film, *The Front Page,* she was as vital and alive as an ingénue. To the end, Helen Hayes refused to consider herself old; instead she referred to herself as a "maturian."

A few years later Becky and I played host at a journalism awards dinner to Malcolm Forbes, a man who in his later years rode a motorcycle and sailed in hot air balloons. Forbes never stopped working and enjoying. After that dinner, he rushed to London to play bridge with members of Britain's House of Lords. Forbes passed away, unexpectedly, only a few days later. In death, he was still full of life. His memorial service in New York was punctuated by laughter.

Since Becky and I retired from our work lives in Washington, the telephone doesn't ring as often, our mail has shrunk to bills and catalogs, and there are fewer social invitations. Elton John no longer sends flowers (he once did for a favor rendered him), and it's been years since the chief justice of the U.S. Supreme Court gave us a commemorative wine tray. Ted Turner no longer gets Becky drinks at media dinners or bargains for her uneaten desserts, and I'm no longer invited to be the Dalai Lama's luncheon companion. That's just a sampling of the hoopla we retired from, and we don't miss the attention.

Too many people reach the end of their lives regretting having missed what might have been. "I could have been a contender," they insist, but gave up the fight long before the bell. George Eliot had the better wisdom: "It's never too late to be what you might have been."[16] Oscar Wilde, confined to a prison workhouse, discovered that "the final mystery is oneself."[17] That is the mystery you now will have the time and leisure to solve, with God's grace to help you.

It is a temptation to become less attached to life in our later years. Resist that temptation. Instead, become more involved with life, and better acquainted with your Creator and Benefactor.

Becky and I have long contemplated renewing our marriage vows. Before beginning this book I refreshed my memory about the promises we made to each other more than a quarter-century ago. It struck me that these are not just vows to be honored between spouses. They are designs for living. Since the moment of our birth we have been wedded to our own lives. If we remain faithful to ourselves and steadfast with those for whom we care, we can look forward to traversing the final seasons of our lives with grace and satisfaction.

From this day forward, resolve to cherish your life—for better, for worse; for richer, for poorer; in sickness and in health; having and holding your blessings; forsaking all that would deter you from your destiny, until death brings new life.

1. From This Day Forward:

Time to Be Courageous

Experience is not what happens to a man.
It is what a man does with what happens to him.
—Aldous Huxley[1]

Be made new in the attitude of your minds . . . put on the new
self, created to be like God.
—Ephesians 4:23-24

"Think of all the poor starving children in Asia," my parents lectured me at the beginning of every Lent in an effort to persuade me to donate part of my allowance to those in need. As adults, even when we choose to make sacrifices, there is still plenty left over to make most of us comfortable. So why aren't we happier as we contemplate celebrating the rest of our lives?

Many of us, in fact, feel worse. Unipolar depression, a condition whose victims always feel downhearted, affects ten times as many Americans today as it did at the end of World War II. Part of the problem with our blessings is the fear that we will lose them. Research reveals that tens of millions of Americans concentrate their attention on worrying about the future rather than enjoying the present. We are prone to complain and feel sorry for ourselves. When we do, we're in no mood to be good to ourselves or anyone else.

The distinction between what we need and what we want has been lost. Most Americans have the necessities. But wants are never satisfied. Dutch researchers estimate that the magic number beyond which money does not buy happiness is just $10,000. What most of us really want from life: affection, companionship, respect, family, and well-being among them, aren't for sale at the mall.

Nor is God's love, which, like hope, is free. As we make plans to celebrate the rest of our lives, we need a circumspect attitude.

Middle age is like Indian summer—a reprise of the waning warm season. It is soon over. Then, as we approach the autumn of our lives, we are confronted with two realities: the dividends from all we have invested of ourselves to date, and our inevitable decline. How we choose to approach the final season of our life on earth determines whether it will be a blessing or a curse. Huxley was right. No one of us can dictate what befalls us in life, but we can decide what to do about it. In this respect we are all invincible.

B. F. Skinner, the founder of behaviorism, lived into his nineties. He focused his research on how people and animals actually behave. In a famous experiment, Skinner trained pigeons to play table tennis—a variation on teaching old dogs new tricks. He proved it could be done.

When he was nearly eighty, Skinner read a paper at the annual meeting of the American Psychological Association titled "Intellectual Self-Management in Old Age," later expanded into a slim book. He recommended welcoming one's advancing years as an opportunity to learn many new tricks. His collaborator, M. E. Vaughan, explains:

Simply put, the enjoyment of life is a by-product of doing something about life. It is only by doing that we experience consequences, and it is the consequences of doing that create an effective enjoyable life. By relying on others to do what needs to be done, we rob ourselves of the effects of these consequences and leave our enjoyment in the hands of others. . . . Unfortunately, feelings often seem to stand in the way of doing, and it often seems that feelings are the hardest things to change. But to change feelings we must first change the conditions that are causing the feelings. The result is feeling better. By doing things that change the particular world you live in, you are able to change what you feel.[2]

There is every reason for the final seasons of our lives to be the most joyful. In his Declaration of Independence, Thomas Jefferson inadvertently misled us: happiness is not an objective to be pursued by divine right. Rather, scientists have confirmed that joy is the by-product of an engaged life. Contented people do not stop to ask themselves, "Am I happy yet?" They are too preoccupied doing whatever it is that commands their attention—whether it be work or family or hobby, or simply doing good for others. Through some still-elusive chemistry, bringing joy to others makes us happy as well.

What Pleases You?
In principle, everyone seeks happiness, but in practice it's the rare person who consistently takes the trouble to enjoy himself or herself. Most of us settle for less than we're due because we don't make the effort. Of course, unless we know what pleases us, we won't be fulfilled, so the rest of your life should be a time of experimentation.

I know men and women who look forward to retirement as an opportunity to fill their days with golf, tennis, or travel. But these pastimes can't possibly fill every day of the rest of one's life. Indeed, single-minded activities will actually shrink your life rather than expand your enjoyment.

For all their talk of sports and cruises, what most Americans *actually* do in retirement is watch television—an average of nearly seven hours every day.[3] Television watching requires no effort and makes no demands. It is pure passive consumerism, certainly not what Skinner had in mind about "doing things that change the particular world you live in." A country club membership won't do the trick either. Rather, you must cultivate an approach and appreciation of life that feed your spirit and keep it full and young. Granted, there is no fountain of youth. There *is* a fountain of aging, however, but you must make the effort to drink from it.

Baby boomers profess a desire to retire early—at fifty-five if they can afford it—yet four of every five plan, if possible, to work at least part-time after retirement. Their motivation is not entirely financial. (The poverty rate among older Americans is 10 percent—the lowest of any segment of the population. By contrast, one of every five children is poor.) Rather, they enjoy activity and recognize that work does not have to be financially remunerative to be satisfying.

Horace Deets, longtime leader of the AARP, announced his retirement at age sixty-three. He is typical of his generation in seeking satisfaction by choosing to be active in his later years. For many years I collaborated with Horace in educating the nation's print and television journalists about the challenges and opportunities for aging Americans. Deets insists that the very idea of retirement is changing: "I think that the biggest change is that retirement, instead of announcing the termination of work, is going to become a time of transition. So you're going to retire from one job and promptly move to another. Or to another career."[4]

He looks forward to the opportunity to control more of his time: "But I'm going to keep working at something. I mean, I don't play golf, I don't own a rocking chair, I get bored very easily, and there are a lot of things I would like to do. But I would also like to have more flexibility in my life."[5]

Deets admits that he contemplates a "phased" retirement: "But I think the worst thing I could do would be to withdraw from all work. . . . Maybe it's part of my Catholic school upbringing that one of the great sins is to squander potential."[6]

At present, only 18 percent of men and 9.8 percent of women are still working at age sixty-five, but there are plenty of definitions of work that don't involve a regular paycheck, and boomers will embrace them when they reach retirement.[7]

Myths of Aging

Youth does not prepare us for aging, so we need to consult the testimony of those who have already negotiated the latter years of their lives. Unfortunately, myths abound, among them that

- Older people think more slowly.
- Their intelligence declines.
- They gain wisdom.
- They need less of everything.
- Old people die of old age.

To be sure, by the age of seventy the brain shrinks to about half its former size, but it works just as well.[8] Psychologists are inclined to blame forgetfulness in older people on the fact that they have lived so long that their minds are like crowded attics, where treasures are easily misplaced but not lost.

Experience doesn't automatically translate into wisdom. In fact, as we age, we are tempted to become "set in our ways" altogether, halting the learning process. Those who succumb to a life of repetition are condemned to viewing life in black and white rather than in living color.

We would all be wise to heed Thoreau's counsel to "simplify, simplify, simplify" in this time of our lives.[9] But as we age we need more, not less, of everything (just look in my medicine cabinet!).

As for dying of old age, it's a total myth. As Henry Ford discovered about his own Model T, even a complicated machine doesn't just wear out. Rather, one component stops functioning. Contrary to expectations, the Rand Corporation discovered that "people under the age of fifty-five are getting sicker, while everybody above that age is getting relatively healthier."[10] It is because younger Americans' lives are more stressful than ever, while their elders can relax and take advantage of improved health maintenance. Hippocrates believed maturity wasn't reached until the age of fifty-six. Aristotle reckoned that the soul did not reach perfection until one turned fifty—twelve years *beyond* the average life expectancy in ancient Greece![11]

Maturity

The National Council on Aging discovered that Americans in the spring and summer of their lives have notions about aging that do not square with the actual experience of those who have reached their autumn. For example:

- Approximately 62 percent of young people believe seniors have serious problems making ends meet. Only 15 percent of older Americans agree.
- Sixty percent believe seniors are afflicted with loneliness. Only 12 percent of aging Americans concur.
- About 54 percent believe aging Americans do not feel needed. Just 7 percent of seniors agree.

- More than half of young people believe those over sixty-five have "very serious problems" with poor health, but only one in five older Americans will admit to it.[12]

In the industrialized world today, the sixty-five-and-older population is 14 percent. It will *double* in the next thirty years. By 2030 the number of men and women eighty-five and older will have *tripled*. Nearly a third of the population of the developed countries will be in their later years as well.[13]

No one outgrows old age, but advanced age of itself does not guarantee maturity, which must be gained through activity. Thomas Jefferson retired from the White House at the age of sixty-six but remained active until his death at eighty-three. Jefferson was so involved throughout his later years that, in the inscription for his tombstone, he neglected to note that he had been president of the United States.

It is widely agreed that our culture worships youth, and it is true that we spend more on cosmetics, diets, and plastic surgery than on alleviating poverty. But, aside from wanting to look and act youthful, we set a greater value on maturity, which can only be achieved with age. The MacArthur Foundation sets three rules for successful aging:

1. Avoiding disease and disability
2. Maintaining mental and physical function
3. Continuing one's engagement with life[14]

To these we must add maturity in spirit. Thomas Moore notes that, "Growing old is one of the ways the soul nudges itself into attention to the spiritual aspect of life. The body's changes teach us about fate, time, nature, mortality, and character."[15]

The mature man or woman is at once active and contemplative, occupied and thoughtful, reverent and fun loving.

Spiritual Maturity

Since Christians believe that all men and women are made in God's image, their quest for maturity is an adventure in which they seek to correspond to the Creator's design for everyone. By the time we reach the later decades, we will have typically embraced safe habits and lowered our emotional expectations. But maturity is something else altogether. It requires emotional growth and the development of new habits.

The word *man* (cf. Latin: *mens*) is derived from an Indo-European verb meaning "to think." To be human one must take thought. It was said that our second president, John Adams, thought about "large subjects largely." In this he was most human. He would write in his diary: "At home with my family. Thinking." and "At home. Thinking."[16]

Our word *adult* comes from the Latin *adolescere*, meaning "to grow up." Mature men and women are those who have grown up by taking thought and being thoughtful. In both classical and Christian civilization, to be mature means to pit reason against the chaotic forces in the world. In our advancing years we have the leisure to find serenity and to be reasonable in our approach to people and circumstances.

Unfortunately, by the time they reach this stage, many men and women have a chip on their shoulders. "The most dangerous weakness of old people who have been amiable," said La Rochefoucauld, "is to forget that they are no longer so."[17] We have all encountered older people who take the attitude that they don't have to be nice to anyone anymore, but can speak their minds. The problem is that what's on their minds is not reasonable, but merely irritable and immature. When we follow in their footsteps, may we be kindly rather than crotchety.

As we age, our physical lives get more complicated, so it is only reasonable to develop good physical habits, streamlining and simplifying our lives. Most people in retirement will have less income than when they were working. That in itself is a spur to simple living. But typically they also have fewer responsibilities placed on them. They usually no longer need to worry about raising children or the demands of a full-time job.

Simplicity is a strategy to jettison other distractions, in order to concentrate on what really satisfies you. Maturity means paying attention to enjoyment—your own and that of others. You can't stop to smell the roses unless you grow roses to smell, and you won't enjoy them if you only think of their thorns.

Clearing the Clutter

Finding satisfaction in the golden years does not come from sugarcoating the realities of growing older, but from clearing away the clutter that keeps us from enjoying simple gifts. Whereas we formerly worked to gain the income to entertain ourselves, now we have the leisure to enjoy things that cost little or nothing—a simple meal that doesn't have to be rushed, a book from the library, a conversation with a friend, an opportunity to help someone in need, a deeper intimacy with those we love, including the God who loves us.[18]

Before he became the Buddha, Prince Siddartha was a pampered boy, confined by his father in a splendid castle. Curious about the world beyond the ramparts, he slipped outside. Driving around the countryside, he saw a withered, toothless old man, mumbling to himself and tottering with the help of a stick. The prince was astonished at the sight and asked his driver whether everyone grows old.

"It is the world's pity," the spoiled prince acknowledged, "that weak and ignorant beings, drunk with the vanity of youth, do not behold old age! Let us hurry back to the palace. What is the use of pleasures and delights, since I myself am the future dwelling-place of old age?"[19]

By confronting the reality of old age and embracing solidarity with all humanity, Prince Siddartha was transformed into the Buddha, who devoted his life to helping others accept the human condition with serenity. In this, he differed from many of our contemporaries, who traverse their later years oblivious to the fact that no one outgrows old age. Serenity comes from accepting its inevitability and the likelihood of decline while still mining the riches of the rest of our lives.

Jesus, unlike the Buddha, died young, never tasting old age. But even as a babe in arms, he prompted the aged Simeon to embrace his own demise with serenity and hope: "Sovereign Lord, as you have promised, you now dismiss your servant in peace. For my eyes have seen your salvation" (Luke 2:29).

It is the genius of Christianity that one man's death gave the promise of eternal life to all humans. Humanity, created in the divine image for God's own pleasure, was offered the certain hope of sharing eternity with its Maker. Christians believe death to be not a period at the end of life's sentence, but merely a comma, introducing a new and eternal story. As Shelley rhapsodized in "Adonais," his tribute to the dead Keats: "Peace, Peace! he is not dead, he doth not sleep / 'tis Death is dead, not he . . ."

Then the poet expressed hope for himself, as well as for you and me:

> That Light whose smile kindles the Universe,
> That Beauty in which all things work and move,
> That Benediction which the eclipsing Curse
> Of birth can quench not, that sustaining Love
> Which through the web of being blindly wove
> By man and beast and earth and air and sea,
> Burns bright or dim, as each are mirrors of
> The fire for which all thirst; now beams on me,
> Consuming the last clouds of cold mortality.[20]

Eternal Youth

Mortimer J. Adler, longtime editor of the *Encyclopedia Britannica*, lived to the age of ninety-eight. He never retired. On his eightieth birthday, he offered this advice to his younger colleagues: "Never work more than seven days a week or twelve hours a day, and sometimes a little less. To grow younger with the years, work harder as you get older."[21] Adler praised active engagement with life. He had the rare capacity to relax into it. Few of us can match him or would care to. Work for him meant an open mind and disciplined life, which can guarantee serenity and satisfaction for a lifetime.

The longest-living, healthiest people in the world live on the island of Okinawa, part of Japan. At present the population of 1.27 million includes 427 men and women over the age of one hundred—four times the rate in western nations. Okinawans age more slowly than Americans. Long-term and fatal illnesses common among us are almost unheard of among Okinawans.

A twenty-five-year study of the island population by doctors Craig and Brad Wilcox and cardiologist Makoto Suzuki reveals that Okinawans have 80 percent fewer heart attacks, physiologically younger arteries, less than one-fourth the incidence of breast, ovarian, and prostate cancer, and only half the hip fracture rate of people in western nations. Menopause occurs a full decade later than in the United States, and its effects are so slight that hormone replacement therapy is unnecessary.

The Okinawans' formula for longevity includes healthy diet and exercise, but the principal ingredient is the absence of stressful living. The Okinawans are surrounded with natural beauty. No one is in a hurry. People smile and offer pleasantries. Cherry Norton, writing in the *Sunday Times* of London, found the laid-back lifestyle hard on her deadline journalism. "My first encounter with 'Okinawa time' came when I asked someone to help me find some centenarians to talk to," she reports. "They said it would take at least a month or two."[22]

A World Health Organization report on aging concludes that "an increase in longevity without quality of life is an empty prize." Chaiko Asato, 102, agrees. Her secret for a long life: "To live joyfully, to be open-minded, and not to hurry anywhere." She wakes each day at seven, takes a brisk half-hour walk, and plays croquet with friends three times a week. Americans typically wait for a summer vacation week at the beach to enjoy a sunset. Okinawans gather on their island's beaches every night to watch the sun go down.[23]

Making Yourself Sick

Frenetic living is largely a disease of American manufacture. I have lived and worked in France and Italy, where the pace of life is slower and the level of enjoyment is higher. When I was studying for a graduate degree in Paris in the 1960s, I came down with scarlet fever late in the spring term and was bedridden for weeks. Determined to get my degree, I literally dragged myself to examinations. My French classmates were dumbfounded. "Why are you so hard on yourself?" they asked. "There is always next year."

For Okinawans, there is always tomorrow. In the Okinawan dialect there is no word for retirement. People work well into their eighties and nineties, but they are casual about time. Punctuality is not a virtue. Bus schedules are loose. Natives routinely turn up for meetings, weddings, and parties an hour late. In this respect, they are different from the disciplined, workaholic mainland Japanese. Revealingly, young Okinawans who convert to Western lifestyles suffer from Western ailments.

Tege (pronounced tagay) is another ingredient in the island's stress-free lifestyle. It means "half-done." The rule is to do as much as you can without getting overwrought or uptight. "It gives the message that people should not worry too much and they can live harmoniously if they do their best," says Fumiko Oshiro, a forty-seven-year-old office worker.

Okinawa suffers a higher divorce and unemployment rate than the rest of Japan, yet the natives accommodate those difficulties in their lifestyle. They tend to marry young, and marital breakups are accepted philosophically. Divorced spouses remain close to their former in-laws and are welcomed back home by their own parents. Households are multigenerational, and personal loss and emotional ordeals are shrugged off as exceptions in life. For Okinawans of all ages, life's glass is never half empty, but always at least half full.

Okinawans live slowly and avoid fast food. The typical diet consists of tofu, vegetables, fish, fruit, pork, rice, and other whole grains. On a typical day, they enjoy seven servings of fruit, whole grains, and vegetables, and two of soybean products. Fish is eaten three times a week.

Centenarian Chaiko Asato lost both of her parents during World War II and was shot in the leg while she was in hiding during the Okinawan campaign. Today, surrounded by her family, she celebrates her longevity every day. On her ninety-seventh birthday, young Okinawans came to touch her in a ceremony called *ayakaru*, praying to share in her good fortune, health, and many years.[24]

The Virtues and Vices of Age

While most Americans aspire to a long life, we want it to be healthy. Unfortunately, modern medicine has increased our average life span without ensuring the quality of our lives after we reach retirement age. My wife and I are typical of many Americans who have filed living wills with their lawyers, to ensure against doctors prolonging their lives artificially during terminal illnesses.

Today Americans are ambivalent about age. Little more than a century ago, aging was viewed as a natural process, and older people as winners in the survival of the fittest. But before the turn of the twentieth century, attitudes changed. Old age began to be treated as a distinct period of life characterized by decline, weakness, and redundancy, and denigrated as a condition of dependency and deterioration. As gerontology became a science, the wisdom previously associated with age was replaced by studies of senescence.

In preindustrial society, people did not think in terms of childhood, adolescence, and old age. Sociologist Tamara Hareven notes that "children were treated as miniature adults, gradually assuming adult roles in their early teens and entering adult life without a moratorium in their youth. Adulthood flowed into old age without institutionalized interruptions. The two major adult roles—parenthood and work—generally stretched over an entire lifetime without an 'empty nest' and compulsory retirement."[25]

In the past, older people continued to control family purse strings, delaying the financial independence of their children and ensuring themselves a bargaining position for their own support in later years. It was not uncommon for wills to require heirs to support a widowed mother or grandmother. Illness or poverty often made elders financially dependent on children and other kin. When family responsibility failed, town authorities placed the aged in the households of neighbors and even strangers, not in institutions. The poorhouses of the nineteenth century, products of industrialization and urbanization, served people of all ages, not just the elderly.

As today's parents reach retirement, they have typically graduated from child rearing and have a full season of life ahead of them. Today, by dint of marrying and starting a family later, many women still have children at home when they reach middle age. Only a century ago parenthood was a lifelong career due to relatively late marriage, short life expectancy, and greater fertility. Few households were empty nests. In the nineteenth century what we consider the normal life sequence for women—marriage, motherhood, survival with spouse through childbearing years, and widowhood—applied to only 44 percent of women born in 1870 who survived to their mid-teens. The greater majority either died young, never married, were childless, or had their marriages broken by divorce or their spouse's death.

A century ago, fewer than 5 percent of men and women lived alone. Old people made a point of staying in charge of their households. In 1850, nine in ten Americans over the age of sixty-five were still either head of household or spouse. By the 1960s, three-fourths of older Americans were living alone or residing with nonrelatives. Whereas it was once common for aging parents to insist that an adult child postpone marriage in order to care for them, solitary living in old age is now the dominant trend.

It is fashionable to lament the dissolution of the family through divorce, but families today live apart in any case, and parents can no longer rely on the financial support of adult children in old age. Instead they rely on pensions, investments, insurance, and Social Security—all relatively modern contrivances to weather the rest of their lives. Today only one in ten older Americans is considered officially poor, whereas less than a century ago one-fourth of Massachusetts residents over the age of sixty-five were dependent on charity.[26]

Sociologist Erik Erikson believes that the increasing segmentation of life stages and generations in America obscures a deeper problem: "As we come to the last stage (old age), we become aware that our civilization really does not harbor a concept of the whole of life. . . . Any span of the cycle lived without vigorous meaning, at the beginning, in the middle, or at the end, endangers the sense of life and the meaning of death in all those whose life stages are intertwined."[27]

Adding to Your Life

Clichés are tedious precisely because they are true. As you age it becomes even more appropriate to greet each new day as the first day of the rest of your life. Just because you are free of some of the burdens you have carried through your middle years does not guarantee success in your later years. Once you subtract child-rearing and paid employment from daily living, you will need to concentrate on what *additions* to make in their stead.

Every Sunday on our way to worship, Becky and I pass a billboard advertising the Virginia Lottery. In huge print it states the size of the current jackpot. In very small print it reveals that anyone's chance of winning it is one in 135 million! That revelation offers a powerful subject for meditation: if my religious faith and hope enjoyed such slim chances of being true, I would have cause to despair.

If there were a freedom of information act that covered the nation's lotteries, it would reveal that the vast majority of big winners fail to find happiness. In fact, most run through their money and wind up much as they started. Winning the lottery is simply not the great new lease on life that it's cracked up to be. The reason is revealing: big winners typically quit work altogether and start spending on luxuries—cars, homes, and vacations. In the process, they leave family, friends, and familiar surroundings behind, embracing a self-imposed exile.

It doesn't take much imagination to realize that winners are actually *poorer* for the freedom the lottery afforded them, because they left behind proven sources of happiness for hollow consumerism. Your retirement years will be an opportunity for engagement, not escape—not for a life of doing *nothing*, but for a fuller life of activity doing something satisfying: richer occupation, deeper education, sounder health, a more positive attitude, and a workable faith. It is a time for loving, savoring, and celebrating—not declining. You can't purchase what you will need with lottery earnings, but only with imagination and effort.

Before they graduate, Dartmouth College seniors are each asked to write an essay answering the question, "What would you do if you had a million dollars?" Afterward each is asked, "How could you accomplish the same goals without the million dollars?" Revealingly, most graduates devise a workable plan, illustrating the fact that we don't have to invest money in our happiness—only ourselves.

Attitude

The mark of a good card player is the ability to win with a bad hand. Life deals everyone lousy cards once in awhile; the trick is to know when to hold 'em and when to fold 'em. If until now you have folded too quickly, you will now have the opportunity to play more aggressively. The key is a positive attitude. At most, only half of your life's quality is dictated by the facts; the other half is controlled by your attitude. With a positive, realistic approach you can *change* the facts.

But first you must face the facts and see them for what they are. A stiff upper lip in the face of adversity is the way of retreat and denial. Anger and mourning are better attitudes. If you don't think so, recall Jesus driving the moneychangers from the temple and weeping at the tomb of his friend Lazarus. If Christ could show strong emotion in adversity, so can we.

Neither optimism nor pessimism will get us anywhere at this stage in our lives, because they fail to reflect reality. It is as foolish to believe that your life will get better without effort as it is to believe that it is bound to get worse despite your efforts. Your investment *of* yourself *in* yourself makes the difference.

When the class of 1953 graduated from Yale University, only 3 percent of its members expressed clear goals for life after college.

Twenty years later those few classmates were earning more money than the other 97 percent combined! They were no brighter than the rest, only more focused and persistent. Money isn't the only measure of success, of course. Vincent Van Gogh sold only one painting in his entire lifetime, but he never abandoned his art. No one can call him a failure.

F. Scott Fitzgerald, whose *The Great Gatsby* is often hailed as the Great American Novel, alleged that "there are no second acts in America."[28] He was wrong, as his own life demonstrated. After the death of his wife, Zelda, and his decline into alcoholism, Fitzgerald found a second career as a screenwriter in Hollywood and a new love. In 1953, at a time when it appeared that the world might suffer a nuclear holocaust, William Faulkner in his Novel Prize address predicted that, by dint of the resilient human spirit, humankind would not only survive but also prevail. With the end of the Cold War, he was proven right. While survival is the best revenge against adversity, success is even better. It will not be thrust upon us; rather, our success will be of our own making.

Confidence

One photo in the Yount's family album is unlike all the others. It was taken by an Associated Press photographer and ran on the front pages of newspapers around the world. It shows Becky hugging her godfather, Jeremy Levin, at Andrews Air Force Base outside Washington at the end of his long ordeal as a hostage in Lebanon. Jerry, then CNN bureau chief in Beirut, was the first American to be taken hostage and the only one to actually escape his captors. Through his long months in solitude, chained to a radiator, he had no contact with the outside world. Inexplicably, his Muslim captors provided Jerry, a Jew, with a New Testament. It became his anchor, giving him hope and supporting his sanity.

Shortly after his liberation, I invited Jerry to lunch at the National Press Club. Still gaunt, shaken, and plagued with nightmares, he nevertheless refused to assume the role of victim. Like people surviving near-death experiences, he felt transformed. Because of his ordeal, life had become inexpressibly precious to him. Jerry would be the last to claim that he was a better person for his ordeal, but he felt grateful and confident for the future. Ever since, he has worked for reconciliation between the Israelis and Muslims. Where he could have been expected to harbor hate for his captors, he learned to love them.

Few of us are taken hostage, but we are all confronted with challenges and personal losses that we carry with us into the final season of our lives. A person who loses his job or whose marriage ends in divorce does not feel better because he knows of others who suffer more. More often, we shrink from our tragedies and attempt to insulate ourselves from further hurt. Instead of affirming life, we feel threatened by its fragility, and we lose confidence.

For many people, self-confidence can only be achieved through a kind of transcendence. The author Graham Greene, who was subject to deep depression, considered his writing to be a form of therapy. He wondered "how all those who do not write, compose, or paint, can manage to escape the madness, the melancholia, the panic fear which is inherent in the human situation."[29] Bruno Bettelheim, studying life in the Nazi concentration camps, observed that the first to die were those who abandoned any attempt at controlling their destinies and felt helpless in the hands of their captors.

Transcendence requires participation in recovery, not capitulation to challenge. Confidence rests on faith in something beyond yourself. If you conceive of yourself merely as an accidental speck of life in a vast, impersonal universe, you will not be likely to find a faith that holds out much hope as you negotiate your later years. Believers and doubters are equally exposed to life's trials, but believers know where they stand in the universe and where they are going.

If you or I attempted to live confidently on the basis of what we absolutely know for a fact, we could never get out of bed in the morning to face the uncertain day. People cannot help but live by faiths that fall short of absolute certitude, but we can shed false faiths that are built of little more than habit and sentiment.

In the century recently ended, more than 100 million men, women, and children died miserably and prematurely in time of war, the victims of false faiths—fascism and communism—that turned their adherents into self-righteous killers. By contrast, a good faith is not righteous, but honest and humble, generous and true. It takes no prisoners and claims no victims. Believing in yourself rests on believing in something beyond yourself. For the vast majority of Americans of all ages, that something is God. Develop a faith that will sustain you through the rest of your life. Test it and deepen it. From this day forward, live from your faith.

2. Forsaking All Others:

Be True to Yourself

What a man thinks of himself,
that is what determines,
or rather indicates, his fate.
—Henry David Thoreau[1]

Search me, O God, and know my heart;
test me and know my anxious thoughts.
—Psalm 139:23

The United States is the only nation that claims happiness to be its citizens' God-given right. But according to the World Database of Happiness, Americans barely make it into the top ten of the world's industrialized nations in terms of life satisfaction. Overall, the natives are happier in Iceland (#1), the Netherlands, Sweden, Switzerland, Denmark, Ireland, Belgium, and Great Britain as well as down under in Australia.

The problem is that, much as we seek it, happiness can't be purchased, and it's hardly serendipitous. The leading expert in the "science of well being," Professor Martin Seligman of the University of Pennsylvania, believes there are three kinds of happiness: "the pleasant life," the joy that comes from eating, drinking, sex, and entertainment; "the good life," which derives from enjoying things you do well; and "the meaningful life," which consists of devoting yourself to something you believe in. The secret to true happiness comes from combining good and meaningful living. He dismisses the satisfaction of the senses as merely "whipped cream with the cherry on top."

Seligman and his fellow scientists believe there are reasons to be cheerful, among them: being born into a happy family; developing a positive attitude; being married; socializing; volunteering; and living a religious faith. Jesus affirmed as much in his Sermon on the Mount when he pronounced even the poor, the sorrowful, the just, the merciful, the persecuted, and the peacemakers to be happy (Matthew 5:3-11). We, too, can claim happiness as we celebrate the rest of our lives.

In the spring of 1845, the young Thoreau went into the Massachusetts woods and, with a borrowed axe, made himself a home on the shore of Walden Pond in which he lived for two years and two months. "My purpose in going to Walden Pond," he explained, "was not to live cheaply nor to live dearly there, but to transact some private business with the fewest obstacles."[2]

That private business was to learn about himself. The purpose of his adventure was to establish his own values and agenda, rather than patterning his life according to others' expectations of him. He believed that, by thoughtless conformity, most men and women "begin digging their graves as soon as they are born."[3]

To this day his warning causes me more than a little discomfort. I have already enjoyed a life a quarter-century longer than the hermit of Walden Pond, yet remain ill acquainted with myself and less content than I should be. Thoreau prefaced his account of his sojourn in the woods by acknowledging that, "I should not talk so much about myself if there were anybody else whom I knew as well."[4] He was a fortunate man to possess such self-knowledge.

In our later years, it's likely that our daily routines will no longer be subject to the expectations of work or child rearing. We can look forward to retirement not only from the demands of steady wage-earning but also from the supervision of our lives by others. We do not quite become masters of our fate, of course, yet we will be in possession of our lives as never before and must learn to supervise them. Most of us will not have parents, teachers, or supervisors to set our agendas for us for our remaining years—*we* will need to do it for ourselves.

Among the difficult sayings of Jesus were those in which he insisted that his followers must break away from the familiar and routine. Consider Jesus's instruction to the rich man in Mark's Gospel: "One thing you lack," he said. "Go, sell everything you have and give to the poor, and you will have treasure in heaven. Then come, follow me" (Mark 10:21). Jesus promised his followers that "no one who has left home or brothers or sisters or mother or father or children or field for me and the gospel will fail to receive a hundred times as much in this present age . . . and in the age to come, eternal life" (Mark 10:29-30).

We cannot navigate our mature years by following the paths of our youth or even middle age. Instead you and I must march to a different drummer—and we are that drummer. "Our life is frittered away by details," Thoreau lamented as he distanced himself from cares inflicted on him by others. "The mass of men lead lives of quiet desperation."[5]

Critic Michael Dirda acknowledges that Thoreau's voice "whispers to me in the still sad mornings when I waken and wonder, like many other people: Have I missed my life? Sacrificed my soul to the gods of this world? Chosen the safe path, when I might have taken the thrilling and dangerous one?" He wonders, "When did I stop hearing the music that was playing just for me?"[6] It is never too late to make your own acquaintance. Thoreau invites us to: "Go forth on the shortest walk, perchance, in the spirit of undying adventure, never to return—prepared to send back our embalmed hearts only as relics to our desolate kingdoms." He adds: "If you are ready to leave father and mother, and sister, and wife and child and friends, and never see them again—if you have paid your debts, and made your will, and settled all your affairs, and are a free man, then you are ready for a walk."[7]

To Thine Own Self Be True

"By Thoreau's standards," Dirda admits, "few of us are ever ready for a real walk. But who knows? Maybe one of these dawns I'll finally set out."[8]

But we set out only to return a more autonomous and involved person. Jesus went into the desert for forty days and nights and then rejoined life with a clear mission. Mohammed went to the mountain and then returned transformed. Prince Siddartha retreated from life only to find the wisdom to lead others to serenity. Thoreau himself became "a sojourner in civilized life again" after twenty-six months in the woods to share his wisdom with the rest of us.[9]

We can be tempted to associate the quest for self-discovery with an adolescent urge to escape responsibility. But what you and I want to achieve during the retirement years is not escape but confrontation with ourselves, followed by commitment to others. Short of that, we will be vulnerable to quiet desperation as our lives wind down.

Rest assured, self-knowledge is not self-indulgence. The better you know yourself, the better you will be for others, because only those who own themselves can give of themselves. And the better you will be for yourself, because you will know what gives you true satisfaction and what is bogus and a waste of time.

If you are privileged to celebrate your later years in the company of a life partner whom you love, then you have already forsaken all others for your spouse. But retirement can be hard on a marriage unless partners allow each other space and autonomy. If you have encountered difficulties agreeing on vacations, meals, and entertainment up till now, your preferences can become divisive as each of you ages. Couples who do not worship together are nearly half as prone to breakup than those who share the same religious faith.[10]

My wife Becky tells me there are two tests a couple must pass to prove their compatibility: they must be able to enjoy the same activities on vacation, and they must be able to hang wallpaper together without wanting to kill each other. We're fine together on vacation, but thank goodness we hired a professional to hang our wallpaper so we weren't put through the second test!

Valuing Your Better Half

It is easier to confront others than to face yourself. Before the massacre of the Albigensian heretics in the thirteenth century, a soldier asked his bishop: "Whom should I kill, and how can I distinguish between Catholics and heretics?" The bishop counseled: "Kill them all. God will know his own."[11]

We are better advised as we contemplate the rest of our lives to develop our own good judgment rather than leaving it to heaven. There are heresies in our own character and behavior, and only honesty with ourselves will ferret them out and open the path to our redemption. In the *Star Wars* films the heroes relied on the Force within themselves to defeat the powers of darkness. Christians rely on God's indwelling Spirit to clear us of our contradictions and build our integrity.

A loving spouse can help us to be honest with ourselves. When I am required to introduce myself before a lecture, I say that "I am Rebecca Yount's husband"—not only because I am proud of her, but also because she is truly my better half.

Outside of armed combat in the field, marriage is the most honest, confrontational relationship any man or woman is likely to experience in life: "Husband and wife see each other not only with their pants down but with their guards down and their makeup off. Sentimentality and passion rarely provide enough sticking power to sustain an eyes-wide-open relationship, and children are often only a diversion. It takes a lot of love and humility to keep committing oneself to a spouse who has seen us at our worst."[12]

Becky calls me a "high maintenance husband" even now, but I was worse in the summer of my life, burdened with chronic insomnia and nervous depression, combined with frequent respiratory infections and male midlife craziness. When my doctor prescribed a state-of-the-art drug for my sleeplessness, the medication produced episodes of peevish, argumentative, violent, and unreliable behavior, along with total memory loss. I awoke every morning feeling utterly innocent, to be told by Becky and our children what a monster I had been the night before. Getting the bad news was a minor embarrassment but a major blessing, because I was forced to take responsibility for my behavior and change it. Happily, I kept my wife.

But it's unfair to treat your spouse as an unpaid therapist. Friends, other family members, or a professional counselor can be recruited to help us confront ourselves.

Becky's harshest judgment on difficult but sensitive people is to tell them, "You can dish it out, but you can't take it." She has used that line on me, with withering effect, and I have borrowed it from time to time to confront a few martinets on my own.

We are all too quick to forgive ourselves and too slow to forgive others. Self-knowledge has the happy effect of making us more tolerant of others' faults and inconsistencies. It makes us aware that we are not perfect but need forgiveness. Self-knowledge allows us to drop our poses and become friends with ourselves, warts and all. Humility is a virtue because it allows us to face the truth about ourselves.

But don't start confronting yourself if you think you're a worm and a failure. You'll only become more depressed. Find a reliable therapist or coach to nurture you through the healing process. Confrontation only works when you have a basically good (or at least neutral) opinion of yourself. No one of us is either as wonderful or as awful as we imagine. Happiness comes to those whose self-scrutiny is simply an honest and friendly unburdening of illusion and pretense.

The Hollywood Curse

Hollywood is hard on aging, and audiences tend to believe what they see on the silver screen. Gloria Swanson was only fifty when she played the role of Norma Desmond in *Sunset Boulevard*, but she was made to look and act like a crone. Few actresses are allowed to grow older gracefully. Think of Joan Crawford and Bette Davis in *Whatever Happened to Baby Jane?* or Katherine Hepburn in *The Lion in Winter*—for which she won an Oscar—or the actresses in the film *Searching for Debra Winger*.

Lillian Gish and Helen Hayes gave themselves permission to age naturally without trying to turn back the years, but their close friend Greta Garbo chose to become a recluse rather than allow herself to be revealed as someone older than the glamorous Camille. In later years, Marlene Dietrich isolated herself in her Paris apartment, hoping fans would remember her for her former beauty.

Hollywood's leading men fare better as they age, retaining romantic roles long past the time they are credible lovers of much younger women. Think of Robert Redford, Richard Gere, Warren

Beatty, Clint Eastwood, Michael Douglas, and Sean Connery, playing opposite actresses less than half their age. Believing their own publicity, some of them favor younger women off-screen as well. Somehow these men are able to pull off the illusion of agelessness. Cary Grant never lost his youthful charm.

There is a lesson here, and I suspect it is that attractiveness is a matter of attitude and vitality. Age may not be an asset, but it is not a liability. If Clint Eastwood still thinks of himself as Dirty Harry and Sean Connery still feels James Bond in him, then audiences are inclined to go along with the pretense. Recall that Thoreau affirmed that one's self-knowledge indicates one's fate. Unless one's sense of self is hopelessly inflated, we tend to accept a person's self-estimation.

Some women refuse to allow age to change the public's perception of them. In separate polls, Diana Rigg and Sophia Loren were voted the sexiest women in the world when in their sixties. In her thirties, Isabella Rossellini was fired as the face of a cosmetics firm for being past her prime. She struck back by creating her own cosmetics line of products for mature women. Goldie Hawn and Barbra Streisand successfully defy the years because of their self-attitude and their vitality.

I grew up enchanted with the actress Audrey Hepburn and was privileged to meet her not long before her death from cancer. I found her to be unexpectedly tall, painfully thin, and shy, with crooked, nicotine-stained teeth. But she was clearly the princess of *Roman Holiday*, the gamine from *Sabrina*, and Natasha from *War and Peace*. Despite my admiration for Ginger Rogers's screen portrayals with Fred Astaire, I passed up an invitation to a press luncheon with her because she had misplaced her personality in later years, becoming a caricature of her former self.

That European women refuse to allow age to detract from their attractiveness explains why European men are attracted to older women. Among American women today, Lauren Hutton stands out as an example of a woman who has successfully redefined her appeal as she has aged. Despite a series of physical, financial, and emotional setbacks, the gap-toothed model is still vital, promoting hormone replacement therapy for menopausal women.

As we age, the attractiveness of maturity, life experience, and character trump the mere physical attractiveness of youth.

Playing "Old Person"

In my senior year in college I played the part of an old codger in a musical review—to rave reviews, at least from my friends. I wore a white wig and ragged clothes, stooped, shuffled, trembled, and muttered to myself about the good old days. In real life offstage I was dating the pretty heroine of the play. Only now do I appreciate the irony.

The smiling photo I favor for publicity depicts a person seventeen years younger than I am now. It is gratifying to freeze time thus. But because I host a television show, I cannot pretend to perpetuate the image of a younger David. I inherited my mother's flaming red hair. Unfortunately, redheads do not gray gracefully as they age. The color disappears completely, and I find myself almost as white-haired as the old fella I played in college nearly fifty years ago.

Just as children are judged more leniently by the courts than adults, older people tend to be tolerated despite their eccentricities. Nearly two-thirds of Americans profess to want to live to be one hundred, although only 8 percent expect to live that long.[13] In any case, the longer we live, the more inclined we are to be odd, if not dotty, because there's no one who cares to take the trouble to correct us. Actress Estelle Winwood, still active on the New York stage into her nineties, began to make up her dialogue as she went along, and took to nudity offstage. The English are probably best at being off-center. We know of a woman in Essex who keeps a four-hundred-pound pet pig in her farm kitchen.

B. F. Skinner believed it important that people not drift into the part of old persons, but that we decide beforehand what kind of person we intend to be as we age. A facelift may give you an appearance younger than you are, but it will not arrest age or make you youthful inside. "All the world's a stage," the psychologist affirmed, "and you are not the first to play the part of Old Person. The Old Persons who have walked the boards before you have been crotchety, stingy, boastful, boring, demanding, and arrogant. They have complained of their illnesses and many other things."[14]

Skinner affirmed "how easy it is to play the part that way," especially considering that it is what most audiences expect of older persons. Were these dreary traits in us when we were younger? Probably, but they were not summoned as frequently. It is the *circumstances* of advancing years that tempt us to act the part of the difficult Old Person. But we can rewrite our script. During our later years it will be only realistic to graduate to roles as successful character actors, drawing smiles rather than groans from our audiences.

When Becky and I vacation in England every year and I request senior citizen discounts, I am not allowed to identify myself euphemistically as a senior but must announce myself as an Old Age Pensioner. How humiliating! Still, I go for the discount. Skinner acknowledges that older people are often stingy, tipping less, complaining more about prices, giving cheaper gifts, shrinking their charities. If you continue to tip the cloakroom attendant a quarter when everyone else is tipping a dollar, you are perpetuating an outmoded image of an old person. "If you would play the role of Old Person in modern dress," Skinner advises, "you must learn new lines and new stage business."[15]

In my wife's novel, *A Death in C Minor*, she created two older characters whom I would cherish as friends if they had lives off the printed page. One is Aunt Clare, a blind, childless widow who lives alone but enjoys the company of younger people, maintains a sense of humor, keeps active, and is a joy to be with. She is not just a product of Becky's imagination: we have met many Aunt Clares among mature English women.

The other character is Sir Brian Foley, a retired Army colonel, also widowed, whose only child lives far away in America. The colonel walks with a cane and trembles from Parkinson's disease, but he is the most interesting man in his Essex village, steeped in its history, alert to everything going on. He is a war hero but keeps his war stories to himself. Sir Brian does not suffer fools gladly, but he is the most reliable of friends.

Cicero said that life is a play with a badly written last act. But that does not require that we play it badly or oddly. We will be the same persons in the autumn of our lives that we are now. Only the circumstances have changed, both for better and for worse. Better because we are now free to write our lines; worse because we have been consigned to character roles and a smaller stage.

Still, we can dedicate ourselves to giving good performances, marked with serenity, wisdom, freedom, dignity, and a sense of humor. Serenity is an inward state, but it relies on a tranquil world. As we age, our worlds can become so tranquil that nothing seems to be happening, so we must make it happen. Emerson suggested that as we age we should take in sail; still, we must not allow ourselves to drift.

Growing Older, Acting Young

While aging can limit us in some respects, maturity itself acts as an enabler, keeping us vital both spiritually and physically. Remember, we are made in God's image. Contrary to traditional depictions, God is not old. Rather, God is eternally young. God does not dwell on the past or the future, but on the present. So should we, mining its riches. Regret for the past and anxiety about the future can spoil our remaining years this side of eternity. Instead, we are better advised to celebrate our present blessings, which may require us to cultivate new habits of mind and body.

Men and women look forward to retirement, but many perversely prefer to live in the past once they reach it. Resist the urge to become a bore. Sociologist Alan Wolfe notes that "every generation finds the morality of previous generations better than its own" and accordingly denigrate the present to hallow the past.[16] While the articles in AARP's magazine are upbeat and forward-looking, some of the advertisements in the back pages glamorize the past, promoting recordings from the 1930s, '40s, and '50s before anyone heard of Elvis.

B. F. Skinner explains why older people are bores: "For one thing, they talk too much about the old days. When the old and the people they talked to were both young, those were the new days, and talk about them was talk about current events. Now, what the old talk about seems to their young audiences to be ancient history." Skinner's rule of thumb is this: "Unless asked to do so, do not talk about personal experiences of more than a decade ago."[17]

As we mature, we share fewer interests with younger people. But beware of confining your social life to people your own age: you will bore one another. In my teens, when I picked up dates at their homes, the girls were seldom ready, which meant awkward moments with their fathers trying to find common ground for polite conversation. Now I'm on the other end and need to find topics that interest younger people. You will soon be in the same position. But it's worth the effort.

If you have a hobby or special interest, join an organization that has members of different ages. If you belong to a church, attend the family service and meet younger families. When you start to tell a story, play it safe and ask your friends whether they have heard it before. Becky, who is more than a decade younger than I, instantly sounds the alarm if I repeat a tale.

Once you retire, you will have more occasions to sit in doctors' waiting rooms during the day when most people are at work. I bring a book along to read and wear earplugs to avoid elderly patients' conversations about their ailments. If friends are recovering from illness, it is only polite to ask how they're doing, but after a certain stage in your life you will be asking for trouble if you routinely greet your peers with a hearty "How are you?" You don't want to know, and you shouldn't want to tell either. Keep your aches and pains to yourself.

When older people brag about past exploits, it's like me telling fish stories. The fish is no longer around to prove I caught it. Your obituary will relate your former successes, but by the time it appears, they won't matter. Introduce yourself by what you are doing *now* and what interests you *now*. Don't succumb to becoming a historical figure while you're still alive.

By the same token, resist moralizing. Retirement puts us at a distance from the workaday world and younger generations. Just as we had different standards and fashions than our parents, our own children are likely to march to different drummers. As Skinner suggests, "It is better to grant young people their own standards even if you continue to live by yours."[18]

Finding a Passion

Literary authors envy those novelists who churn out best-sellers known as "beach books"—so called because they offer escapist reading for harried men and women on hasty vacations. Becky writes mystery novels, so she's not one to denigrate the genre. Still, her own reading leans to history. Other people's lives are unfailingly fascinating, and Becky always has a new biography going. She reads me just enough of the texts to make me feel that we have another person sharing our lives with us. Every now and then I pick up a book that I should have read long ago in school and am surprised that it makes my life better now. Make friends with your public library, whatever your taste in books.

If you are attracted to gardening or cooking, you already know that you can make life better by *creating* beauty and pleasure. Nothing is as pleasant as good conversation, but it requires us to have something interesting to talk about. People who have hobbies find time in later life to truly indulge them. I have a friend whose passion is collecting old Coca-Cola memorabilia, another who is a Civil War reenactor. Whatever your passion, indulge it. Expand your life.

Wisdom and Freedom

Ancient Rome was ruled by a senate, a word that means "old." The assumption was that wisdom came with age. To this day many religious denominations rely on "elders" for guidance. Aldermen, who comprise city councils, were originally "eldermen."

For years I have written a syndicated newspaper column in which I attempt to apply religious wisdom to the trials and conflicts that make headlines. Actually it's only my *opinion* and, judging by my mail, plenty of readers don't agree with it and consider me not at all a font of wisdom but just a "wise guy."

One of the disadvantages of living in the information age is that we now have such easy access to data that we are inclined to believe it is all we need to be educated. Wisdom is not a matter of fact, but of judgment. We all need advice. That explains the popularity of Ann Landers, Abigail Van Buren, and the telephone psychics who charge by the minute. As you prepare for retirement, you will want guidance to ensure that you do not stumble. That's probably why you picked up this book.

The wisdom you will want to acquire is the knowledge of how to mature successfully and enjoyably. As the entire population lives longer, it will value that kind of practical wisdom more and more. If you are a wise Old Person, the world will beat a path to your door.

Much is made of the freedom enjoyed by those who have retired—but that freedom is mixed. Most retired persons no longer have to submit to office hours, commutes, and supervision, but they are typically constrained by limited budgets, a constricted social life, and health complaints. St. Augustine welcomed aging as a damper on unruly passion, but that liberty can be overstated. A life of enjoyment requires a zest for living that is passionate.

In Washington, ambition is the abiding passion, and aging politicians are reluctant to leave the stage, because it means giving up power. Over the years I chaired press panels that included elder statesmen from previous administrations and Congresses. They were practically impossible to restrain once they had the microphone, because they retained the same ambitions. Former president Jimmy Carter was wise to *change* the nature of his ambitions when he left office. Today, as a diplomat, peacemaker, and advocate for the poor, he is arguably more effective as a senior citizen than he was in the White House.

Having toiled in career-driven Washington, D.C., for decades, Becky and I became accustomed, on being introduced to new people, to identify ourselves by what we did for a living. Today we resist identifying ourselves by our jobs, because our resumes do not say who we are and what we live for. Being a husband and father is vastly more important to me than any other endeavor, and my religious faith defines my life. Unfortunately, obituaries misrepresent people's lives, identifying them with their careers. Old tombstones used fewer words to better effect: "Devoted husband, loving father, trusted friend."

Reminiscence is fine if your memories are sweet, but not if they are tainted with loss, regret, and remorse. Either way, living on your memories is no way to find tranquility as you age. You need to remain active and to keep growing. Serenity is a product of knowing what you like, value, and believe, while embracing life as an adventure with new revelations in store.

Dignity and Humor

Dignity is one of the virtues of old age, but only if we accept the aging process. You probably remember a time, in middle age perhaps, when members of the opposite sex no longer gave you a second look. Younger people attempt to flatter their elders by proclaiming, "You don't look your age." It is better to acknowledge that this is the way a person your age looks.

Admit to your age. Admit it to *yourself* and you will maintain your dignity. Strom Thurmond was already in his nineties when he was guest of honor at a luncheon for some twenty lobbyists. No sooner had I introduced the senator than he spilled an entire bowl of tomato soup in his lap. He skipped not a beat but kept conversing for ninety minutes as if nothing had happened. Just before a two-hour live teleconference I moderated, Lawrence Eagleburger (later secretary of state) spilled a cup of hot coffee in his own lap. Required to answer callers on the air in real time, he made no complaint but kept his dignity.

Dignity requires a sense of humor, because it can only be achieved in the face of the absurd. It's best to laugh at yourself before others find you comical. President Ronald Reagan made an art of self-deprecation, disarming his critics by humorously acknowledging his own embarrassments and misadventures. As we age, we become more prone to gaffes and pratfalls. The best prescription for infirmities is to laugh at them.

People confined to wheelchairs do well to propose wheel-chair races. When aging comics Sid Caesar and Dom DeLuise, both wheelchair-bound, found themselves on the same New York to Los Angeles flight, they challenged each other to race to the baggage area. Dom won by a nose. The lesson of the Special Olympics and competitions between physically challenged adults is that no one is a loser who makes a game of life.

Television favors situation comedies because humor comes from ordinary people finding themselves in absurd situations. Aristotle noted that, alone among God's creatures, humans laugh and blush. We are wise to nurture the ability to laugh at our own embarrassment.

The advancing years bid us to shed solemnity for lighthearted-ness. Life is serious enough without our getting too serious about it. Better to seek comic *relief* from it. As I get older I find dramas tedious and seek out comedies, however contrived. When *Saturday Review* editor Norman Cousins was stricken with a pain-ful, life-threatening illness, he checked into a Manhattan hotel and watched Marx Brothers movies non-stop. Upon recovery, he lectured to medical students about the healing properties of laughter.

Help Wanted: Heroes
It's widely believed that ours is an age without heroes to emu-late. Sports figures and film stars capture the admiration and imagination of youth, but older Americans find practical role models in increasingly short supply. As you age, who will *you* wish to emulate?

Psychiatrist M. Scott Peck recalls a conference of Christian counselors during which Harvard theologian Harvey Cox read aloud the Gospel account of Jesus being summoned to restore the life of a wealthy Roman's daughter (Mark 5:24-34). While

Jesus was on his way, a woman suffering from chronic bleeding reached out and touched his robe. "Who touched my clothes?" Jesus demanded. The woman stepped up and begged him to cure her, which he did before proceeding to raise the Roman's daughter from the dead.

Cox asked the six hundred Christian therapists to name the person in the story with whom they most closely identified. All but six said they identified with the bleeding woman, the grieving Roman father, or with the curious crowd. Only those half dozen professional healers admitted to identifying with Jesus the healer.

"Something is very wrong here," Dr. Peck insisted: "Of six hundred more or less professional Christians, only one out of one hundred identified with Jesus. Maybe more actually did but were afraid to raise their hands lest that seem arrogant. But again something is wrong with our concept of Christianity if it seems arrogant to identify with Jesus. That is exactly what we are supposed to do! We're supposed to identify with Jesus, act like Jesus, be like Jesus. That is what Christianity is supposed to be about—the imitation of Christ."[19]

Whether baptized in infancy or as adults, Christians believe they have died to their worst selves and have been reborn into the better selves God had in mind when God first conceived of creatures made in God's image and likeness. But they must affirm that new life.

When we retire, most of us will no longer be constrained by the expectations of parents, teachers, employers, or even our adult children. We can be the persons we choose to be. The greatest compliment a person can receive is that the world is a better place because he or she has graced our planet and shared our lives.

You and I have already been blessed with lives longer than those of our ancestors. Now we have the opportunity to acknowledge that grace by gratitude and service to the less fortunate. If you are a Christian, familiarize yourself with Jesus's character and consider his invitation to follow him during your remaining years this side of eternity. The Jesus of the Gospels is not enigmatic. We know how he treated parents, friends, enemies, officials, women, children, strangers, the rich, the poor, and sinners. We know:

- How he acted when confronted by treachery
- How he handled emotion
- When he spoke and when he kept his peace
- When he celebrated and when he denied himself
- How he prayed and what he prayed for
- What he valued and what he despised
- How he regarded violence
- How he loved
- What he thought was worth a miracle
- What he thought was worth dying for

Jesus died a young man but packed a lot of living into his brief years. You do not have to be a Christian to find in him a model for the person you want to be for the rest of your life.

3. For Better, for Worse:

Savor Your Blessings, Find Strength in Affliction

The Lord blessed the latter part of Job's life . . . he saw his children and their children to the fourth generation. And so he died, old and full of years.
—Job 42:12,16-17

Be joyful in hope, patient in affliction, faithful in prayer.
—Romans 12:12

A century ago sociologist Max Weber argued that modern capitalism was born from the spirit of Christian asceticism. In short, self-denial rooted in religion led to hard work and financial success.

Three out of five Americans now work more than fifty hours a week, more than their grandparents in the 1920s. Whereas the average American works just under two thousand hours every year, the typical German now labors 22 percent fewer hours, and the Dutch and Norwegians even fewer. Not only is the European workweek shorter than ours, but also our European neighbors typically enjoy month-long annual vacations plus other holidays.

The declines in working hours in northern Europe coincide almost exactly with precipitous declines in religious observance there. Fewer than one in ten northern Europeans attends church at least once a month. Nearly half never go to church. European majorities told the Gallup Millennium Survey that God did not matter to them at all. By contrast, more than four out of five Americans insist that God is "very important" to them.

As you plan the rest of your life, you will want to jettison workaholism in favor of serenity, prepared for both better and worse, and for God's presence in the rest of our lives.

Late in his life, Vincent Price was widowed and afflicted with Parkinson's disease, emphysema, and arthritis. In an unpublished journal, Price reflected on the better and worse of his life. He affirmed, "I remain concerned about what matters most—the Art of Living. To be neglected by ourselves is to die. To be neglected by others for neglecting ourselves is living loneliness."[1]

The actor's father, toward the end of his own life, complained to his son that being elderly is a miserable period of life physically. But the younger Price insisted that "mentally, there are great rewards. You have an entire lifetime during which, if you have spent your time on Earth profitably, you have accumulated enormous amounts of knowledge. You understand things now as you could not when you were younger. You have gained wisdom and perspective."[2]

Price's affirmation of life consisted in thinking every day of something beautiful: "The garden, the juxtaposition of leaves and plants, the variety of shapes of leaves and shades of green. Those are the things that are really worth cultivating in your life, and you must keep your eyes open for them and keep your imagination open to being surprised."[3]

The vow to embrace the rest of our life "for better, for worse," sounds courageous, but it is only an open invitation to savor simple gifts. At any age people with chronic illnesses have "good days" and "bad days." It is better to enjoy the good days than to rail against fate.

We tend to think of our later years as the season in life when people are most physically challenged. But many men and women are handicapped from childhood and remain challenged all their lives. My maternal grandparents were blind from their earliest years. All three of my daughters were born with disabilities, but have carved out successful and fulfilling lives as adults. Over the years, sensitive to their own handicaps, they have served as volunteers assisting others even less fortunate.

The story of Helen Keller is instructive. She had to be liberated from her sightless, soundless prison into a productive and full adult life. What Helen's senses deprived her of, she compensated for with a brilliant mind and many friendships.

Less familiar is the story of Laura Bridgman, born in 1829 in New Hampshire. Stricken with scarlet fever at the age of two, her convalescence took two years. By the age of five she had stopped talking. In the aftermath of her illness, Laura was left not only blind and deaf, but retained only the slightest sense of taste and smell. Her only direct contact with the outside world was through her sense of touch. It was enough. Laura learned to read Braille and express herself by using a manual alphabet, pressing her fingers into the palm of another's hand. She boasted that she had developed a fifth sense she called "think." Although Laura could not hear her own voice, she learned to speak to others. She lived into late middle age. The psychologist Williams James marveled that Laura, deprived of her senses, nevertheless enjoyed an active and rich mental life. "All sorts of terms can transport the mind with equal delight," he reflected. "The schemes and the systems are what the mind finds interesting."

Critic Louis Menand, reviewing a recent biography of Laura Bridgman, acknowledged that, "from a cosmic point of view, all minds are pathetically underpopulated." But they work instinctively. Laura's life was "worse" from the start; with effort she made it better. So can we in our mature years.[4]

Catching Up with Yourself

A fulfilling life is marked by hope, not resignation. Life is richer, if not materially, then spiritually—and by spirituality I include the mind and the senses. Our later years will be a time for feeling, thinking, and savoring. We will have time for these activities, having graduated from the frenetic life of fast food and fast gratification to one of mature appreciation.

These days, life is pursued so quickly that we seldom catch up with ourselves to make our own acquaintance. Look forward to celebrating the rest of your life not as an extended vacation, but as an opportunity to redefine yourself and cultivate simple pleasures. Start with your home. During our working lives Becky and I couldn't afford traditional or even modern furnishings that matched, but each piece, however inexpensive, was chosen for beauty and comfort. We spend almost all of our working and sleeping hours here now, so we make it pleasant and friendly. Every summer we exchange homes with couples in England, Scotland, or France. It's easy to assess another couple's contentment by the comfort of their homes. Don't settle for worse when, with little effort, you can make your surroundings more pleasant.

When I commuted to work every day, I always carried a collapsible umbrella against an unexpected downpour that would ruin my suit. Today my suits are all on hangers in closets, and I wear comfortable clothes that can stand getting wet. Today I enjoy all kinds of weather, as well as the changing seasons, because I have time to notice nature. To be sure, nature is not benign, but it is fascinating, and we are part of it. It enriches our lives.

Feeling Better

Pursuing an active, appreciative life makes us feel better, not worse. But when we feel bad, no one can force us to feel better just by advising us to cheer up. When I go to my doctor with an ailment, the last thing I want from him is cheery counsel. I want to leave the office with a prescription for a pill that either treats the symptoms or, even better, makes me well.

But a good doctor tells his or her patients *how* to have a body that feels better, which probably involves diet and exercise. B. F. Skinner acknowledged that "Americans take billions of pills every year to feel better about their lives even when their lives remain wretched." We turn likewise to alcohol and mind-bending drugs to cover up or escape our malaise. Skinner advises that the better course is not to change *how* you feel but to improve *what* you feel.[5]

The saints accepted that spiritual growth requires one's concentrated attention. If you and I are to grow spiritually and remain vital physically as we celebrate the rest of our lives, we will probably have to cultivate some new habits and routines. Many of them may appear to be mere products of common sense, but it's human nature to resist change even when it's in our best interests.

Aging persons often become discouraged because physical conditions make them feel inadequate. Although eyeglasses are sold now as fashion accessories, their purpose is to correct failing sight. Whereas canes were once fashionable, today they indicate disability. (No one would confuse my blind grandfather's white cane for Fred Astaire's black one.) For some reason, there is a lingering stigma attached to the use of hearing aids.

People tend to treat the *symptoms* of aging rather than the root causes of their complaints. Witness the array of over-the-counter medications in my own bathroom cabinet. Frustration breeds anger. If someday you can no longer easily thread a needle, get a needle-threader or use a bigger needle. B. F. Skinner's book about enjoying one's mature years is printed in large type—a sensible application of the psychologist's principle of changing one's private world instead of grousing about it. Most popular books today are available in large-type editions.

Taking steps to change the conditions under which you live will not be a retreat from life but an assertion that you are in charge of it. As Robert Browning said, "A man's reach should exceed his grasp/Or what's a heaven for?" Reach to make life better.

Grasping the Initiative

As you age, don't succumb to envying the young. Instead, discover and enjoy the privileges of maturity. Take a lesson from professional athletes. They are forced to retire while still relatively young and often do not know what to do with themselves when they are only in their thirties. Many of my neighbors are military officers who retired after just twenty years' service. Although still in the summer of their lives, many of them puzzle over what to do next. AARP reveals that Americans devote eight times as much attention to choosing their clothes than to planning their retirement.[6] You can't expect to enjoy something you haven't prepared yourself for.

As we mature, we can be prone to be more fearful. The only way to control it is to get the facts about your condition. If you are worried whether you have enough money to live on, talk to a financial adviser. If you are worried about your health, talk to your doctor. My mother was inclined all her life to suspect people of taking advantage of her. In later years her suspicions were magnified at the very same time she tended to be more dependent on those she mistrusted.

Millions of Americans are either born disabled or become so long before they enter retirement. They not only cope personally but also are protected by law. By contrast, aging Americans are often unprepared for impaired functioning, which is typically gradual, but which we tend to equate with helplessness and dependency. Humility is a virtue precisely because it acknowledges the truth about ourselves at any age. When you were younger, you could run to catch a bus. In your retirement, you might not run as fast, but you won't have a bus to catch either. You may become slower, but life will be slower too, and you can pause to smell the roses.

Choosing Better, Not Worse

Someone once remarked that the best is the enemy of the merely good. As we age, we may be inclined to believe that we had it best when we were young. We were more lively, healthy, and physically attractive when we had our whole lives ahead of us. But, frankly, we weren't as smart or experienced as we are now, nor as discriminating about our satisfactions. Don't allow nostalgia to discourage you from planning to make your mature years as enjoyable as possible. There is every reason to become an altogether more attractive person as the years pass.

G. K. Chesterton, a clumsy, forgetful man, once affirmed that anything worth doing is worth doing badly. Golfers on the senior circuit can't compete as well as they did in their prime, but they enjoy the game even more. Anything *worth* doing in the final season of life is something we *deserve* to do, however ineptly. When former president George H. W. Bush parachuted from a plane to mark his eightieth birthday, he set no standards for style. In school and career, our accomplishments were always being graded up or down by others. Now no one is keeping score.

Like an explorer entering *terra incognita*, you will probably need some equipment to ease your way through your later years. More than half of men and women over age sixty-five need glasses. Those who are far-sighted, may do perfectly well with cheap reading glasses from the drugstore or a dollar store. Others invest in a flat magnifier that doubles as a bookmark. Stereotypical or not, when I kept misplacing my glasses, I began wearing them around my neck when I'm in the house. It probably makes me look like an old person, but who's to see? Now I don't have to look for them when I need them.

Older people also need to be sure they see well while driving. Someday you might invest in a pair of prescription *sun*glasses as well.

I have glaucoma, which means there are blind spots I'm not even aware of. Other older people suffer poor peripheral vision. Like it or not, as you age, it may take more effort to be sure you are aware of your surroundings. Think of it as a new adventure. For Americans traveling in England, traffic always comes from an unexpected direction, so street crossings are marked "Look Left" or "Look Right." It's always smart to look around.

In my youth I was accustomed to being around blind people who simplified their surroundings to make them predictable and navigable. One of our daughters has impaired eye-motor coordination. When she was young, we simplified her room to make it less confusing, and put colored stickers on drawers and surfaces so she knew where her things belonged. Older people may need to make similar adjustments to their living space. None of this advice may be relevant to you yet, but it's good to know that later, when it is, you can keep choosing the better over the worse for the rest of your life.

Enhancing the Senses

One-third of men and women who reach the age of sixty have already suffered some hearing loss.[7] Most are reluctant to invest in hearing aids but get upset when they feel they are missing a message. Other technology can help. By using headphones for music, those with hearing difficulty can turn up the volume without disturbing others. Closed captioning on television allows the hard-of-hearing to read the dialogue. Modern telephones also have volume controls. There are other aids as well. Even when I am at the far end of our house I know when someone's at the door because our Scottish terrier barks and dashes toward it.

B. F. Skinner suggests that if you will speak loudly to others, they will automatically adjust to your volume in their own speech, and you won't miss a word they say. When people speak to you inaudibly from a distance or from another room, the only solution is to go to them or have them come to you and speak clearly. When I was a student in Paris I often failed to catch what people were saying to me in French but was more confident when I was speaking, because I could choose my words. Speaking up is a good ploy when your hearing is even slightly impaired.

The senses of taste, touch, and smell can also become less acute as we age. But food can be seasoned and its flavor enhanced by sipping water or wine. If older people maintain good hygiene, they won't be concerned about odor. Older people need to consider how their senses affect their safety. My mother once dozed off while smoking and set fire to her apartment. It was the flames, not the smoke, that roused her. Had she had a smoke alarm, she would have had her sense of hearing to protect her.

As we age, our sense of touch can become less sensitive as well. Some older people choose to put away fragile tableware in favor of unbreakable pieces for everyday dining. And they invest in solid, good-quality kitchen utensils. I've always been nervous about the safety of electric can openers, but a cheap mechanical opener can be a challenge for someone with arthritis or poor sense of touch. A good electric can opener costs a few dollars more and works effortlessly. Fortunately, small kitchen appliances are now being made with a real view to safety, which can only reassure us.

If there is a grim rite of passage into old age, it is probably breaking one's hip, a painful event that often makes an aging person feel no longer competent to move around freely. Old animals get around better than older people, and we would probably move around more safely had we been designed with four legs rather than only two. When you reach your later years, you realize the importance of grasping banisters to keep your balance, wearing rubber-soled shoes, and, above all, moving slowly.

Young hikers and mountain climbers find equipment to keep them from falling to be essential. With a little flair older people can make a cane a fashion accessory. Think of Maurice Chevalier and Douglas Fairbanks Jr., and you will know how to use a walking stick with verve. Think of Charlie Chaplin as the Little Tramp, and you will use one with humor.

Forgetting and Remembering

All these devices help aging persons change the conditions of the world in which they live. Whereas memory loss is considered a symptom of aging, I have been forgetful all my life. My favorite coping mechanism is the self-sticking note. When I think of a task I must accomplish, I either do it immediately or write myself a note and place it somewhere it can't be ignored. If you tend to misplace your keys, simply make extra copies. Don't worry that your forgetfulness indicates dementia. Senility afflicts only 2 to 6 percent of people over age sixty-five.[8]

Albert Schweitzer claimed that the key to happiness is good health and a poor memory. True, it's better to have a selectively poor memory than to be burdened with regret for all of the unpleasant things that have befallen us in the past. But we can't function if we can't summon memories. As we age, we can become like the detective looking for a clue who doesn't have a clue what he's looking for. Life will be worse, not better, for frequent lapses in memory, but there are measures we can take to compensate.

For one, we can mentally retrace our steps, just as we would if we were seeking a lost key. Ponder the context of the lost memory, and the missing piece will often pop up. For example, I can tell by the orchestration that a symphony on the radio is by Brahms, but can't remember which it is. By a process of elimination (no, it's not the first or second symphonies, which I *do* remember), I can usually identify it as the third or fourth.

At any age a failure to recall proper names when you are introducing people is embarrassing to everyone concerned. Before I go to a board meeting or a social gathering, I go over a list of those who are likely to be there, and I take the list with me. In Washington people tend to introduce themselves rather than wait for someone else to remember who they are. It is a gracious and practical practice. If I am with my wife, I confide to her that I can't recall a name. By introducing herself, the others' names come out.

One reason we become forgetful is because we have not paid much attention to memorizing matters of importance. I marvel that Becky, a pianist, can play long compositions without referring to sheet music. Because soloists *must* memorize, they do. But a recent survey of Church of England clergy revealed that most of them could not recall all of the Ten Commandments. [9] (Could that mean they don't obey them?)

Older people may lose their train of thought in conversation and begin to wander. That is good reason for speaking in short sentences. Brief remarks also have the value of making one sound sure of yourself.

It is important at any age to keep focused. Journalist Chalmer M. Roberts tells the story of an old English bishop who misplaced his ticket as he was running for his train. The ticket collector politely waved him on saying, "It doesn't matter." "It *does* matter," the bishop complained. "It does because I don't know where I'm going!"[10] Even in the summer of his life G. K. Chesterton was prone to getting lost in London and had to phone his wife at home to ask her where he was.

During the course of a typical day I probably speak more often to my dog and cats than I do to my wife. As you might imagine, Becky does not take well to occasions when I, unthinking, address her by the name of a four-legged furry pet. I also often confuse my daughters' names. They are not amused. The only remedy for such misnomers is to take thought.

When you become older, don't jump to the conclusion that your difficulties in recalling names, events, and tasks indicate Alzheimer's disease. As we age, our brains are crammed with data, and sorting it out takes time and attention. Rely instead on B. F. Skinner's practical tips for jogging your memory.

Alzheimer's disease is an incurable, progressive illness associated almost exclusively with aging. Former president Ronald Reagan was its most prominent victim. Only a doctor can diagnose whether increasing difficulty with memory suggests the onset of Alzheimer's. Identified early, mild to moderate afflictions *can* be treated, allowing people to get better, stay the same, or at least regress at a slower rate.

Other Remedies to Make Life Better

Many people use a weekly or monthly desk calendar and keep it open in a prominent place so they know what's coming up in their lives. As you age, you might add more reminders—for example, when library books are due. Keep a shopping list next to your refrigerator and add items to it as you think of them. One of the unexpected blessings of a desk calendar is all the blank space available to be filled. It invites you to further plan your life and break out of overly narrow routines. An alarm clock was a necessity when we had to rise every morning to go to work. On retirement you may just awake naturally, but an alarm clock can still be useful to remind us when to call a friend, take frozen food from the refrigerator, or watch a favorite television show. I still set my alarm early because our pets demand to be fed.

If all of these remedies for forgetfulness appear to be only common sense, I agree. But until they become routines we will keep forgetting and can become anxious about missing something important.

Thinking Clearly

In my childhood, when my mother complained that her purse was missing, the first place my father and I told her to look was the refrigerator. Returning home from work or shopping, she usually went first to the kitchen, so we had a reason to suggest looking there first. On occasion, I have been known to open a can and throw the opener in the trash instead of the can top, or to toss the contents of a box in the trash while keeping the box. The fault is inattention, distraction, and muddled thinking.

The solution is to know and rehearse what we are going to do *before* we do it. Athletes do it all the time, mentally visualizing what they will do physically. When I decided to write this book, I was uncertain exactly what I was going to say, but I knew that my purpose was to help people like myself enjoy later life. I didn't put a word on paper until I had a working title in mind and a notion of what would be in each chapter. My research was rich but random, and much of it didn't find its way into the final text. But with chapters in mind, I was able to divide the research to suit the subject of each chapter. In the course of writing a book my mind is a sponge, filing away everything I read or hear that might be relevant to my subject. I write at the same time every day for the same number of hours and aim at two thousand or more words. To be sure, I was still forgetful of other things while I was utterly focused on this book. You can be just as attentive to your own favorite projects.

Visitors to my neighborhood who are frustrated by the ten-mile-an-hour speed limit routinely go much faster but are discouraged by speed bumps that force them to slow down. As we age we will slow down both physically and mentally. That doesn't mean we can't accomplish much of what we did when we were young—only that we must be content with a slower pace. Where once we acted impetuously, now we can give better consideration to what really gratifies us without losing spontaneity altogether.

4. For Richer, for Poorer:

Safeguard Your Financial Future

A feast is made for laughter,
and wine makes life merry,
but money is the answer for everything.
—Ecclesiastes 10:19

If you have not been trustworthy in handling worldly wealth,
who will trust you with true riches?
—Luke 16:11

Each year some 2.3 million American couples wed, spending an aver-
age $22,360 to vow "until death do us part." That's the national
average, mind you, including elopements and tiny chapel ceremonies
that cost virtually nothing, to the Hollywood extravaganzas that cost
millions.

Once you are no longer employed, you are unlikely to be richer but,
with planning, you need not fear being poorer.

Christians are taught to pray confidently for their daily
bread, but when we reach retirement it takes more than prayer
to compensate for the end of our paychecks. Although wages end

abruptly, bills still show up in the mail, so we must prepare to support ourselves for our remaining years with savings from our working life.

The challenge of financing retirement is relatively new. When Social Security was inaugurated in the 1930s, only a minority of Americans lived long enough to collect it. Our parents could rely on a pension for their later years, but baby boomers, with greater job mobility, often do not stay long enough with one employer for their pensions to be vested.

Moreover, expenses increase with inflation, making it difficult to save during our working lives. When I went to a private college in the 1950s, tuition was just $650 a year, scholarships were plentiful, and I had a campus job (paying sixty-five cents an hour!). But putting my own three daughters through college meant taking out a second mortgage on our modest home—borrowing, not saving. To make matters worse, many men and women approaching retirement are financially responsible not only for their children, but their aging parents as well.

As we celebrate the rest our lives, we will march to a different drummer, and the beat is slower. So be it. If we don't allow ourselves to be hurried into decisions by fast-talkers, we needn't be suspicious of them. A little foot-dragging will allow us to set our own pace.

Ironically, advances in medicine have both extended our life expectancy and vastly increased the cost of health care for all those extra years. For anyone planning for retirement, there are two utter mysteries that resist solution: How long will I live? and What kind of medical needs will I develop that must be financed from savings?

The Challenge
The two things you *do* know are how much you earn and how

much you spend. Unfortunately, many Americans live month to month on deficit financing. As I've said before, until I remarried in my mid-forties I was consistently in debt, relying on credit cards to keep my head above water, so I can sympathize with the common predicament. But as life's autumn approaches, it is imperative to save as well as spend. Recently I received an e-mail from a reader of my syndicated column whose husband divorced her in middle age, forcing her to raise her daughters by working two jobs, seven days a week. I congratulated her on her success, but acknowledged that she had achieved it by desperate means no one would choose freely.

In the 2001 Retirement Confidence Survey conducted by the American Savings Education Council, one-fifth of Americans acknowledged that they have not put away a single cent toward retirement. Fewer than one-third reported that they have saved something—but less than $50,000.[1] Fewer than one in four have set aside more than $50,000. As a generation, baby boomers are saving more than their grandparents did, but not nearly enough for the extra years they can expect to live—not to mention maintaining the higher standard of living to which they have become accustomed.

Unhappily, some living expenses actually *increase* after retirement. Even with Medicare benefits, we can expect health care bills, paid out-of-pocket, to consume almost 20 percent of our retirement income. You will have to pay for a supplementary health insurance (Medigap) policy at $100 or more each month. The typical policy helps cover deductibles and co-payments but not the cost of dental care and prescription drugs. If you can afford it, you will also want to invest in an extended care policy that will cover most expenses of home health care or nursing home costs during convalescence. My modest policy costs over $1,200 a year.

If you are fortunate enough to hold life insurance, it is reassuring. But remember, it is really *death* insurance, meant for your survivors. And if you hold a term (as opposed to whole life) policy, premiums will rise precipitously as you get older.

The Response

I approach this chapter warily, because I mean for our retirement years to be the best years of our lives, and here I am putting a price tag on them! Unfortunately, food for the body costs more than food for the soul, and we carry both body and soul into our later years. If we intend the rest of our lives to be more than just gold-*plated*, we must invest for them. It is never too late to start saving and planning.

I opined earlier that the two things we *do* know are what we earn and what we spend. But perhaps I was premature. For starters, you may have more money coming to you than your wage or salary. Both Becky and I received small inheritances when our parents died. They were our incentive to start an investment plan for our later years. You may have a small business on the side, or a talent you can turn into extra income. Don't plan on winning the lottery, though.

At the same time, you may know how much you spend, but do you know where it all goes? Rest assured, budgeting does not mean depriving yourself of things you need and want. It means taking a look at your outlays and asking yourself whether they represent the things that matter the most to you. Since we married, Becky and I have kept track monthly, by credit card and checkbook, of every dollar we have spent by category, e.g., food, mortgage (now paid off), household, clothing, autos, utilities, entertainment, and dining out.

Over time we have learned, for example, that we spend more on our pets than on our cars, and more on books and subscriptions than on eating out. Fine. Our pets give us more pleasure than our autos, reading is our passion, and Becky is a good cook. Your priorities will be different; but only by tracking what you spend will you know whether your spending matches your priorities. I can promise that once you know exactly what you are spending, and for what, you will begin to adjust your outlays and discover painless ways to save.

If you are married, your spending must reflect shared as well as individual priorities. Becky goes to a hairdresser and spends just $20 a visit. I haven't visited a barber in thirty-five years (what little hair I have, I cut myself). When our cleaning woman raised her rates a couple of years ago, we agreed to divide housecleaning equally between ourselves. We are not fond of the labor, but have to admit the house has never looked so attractive.

What Will You Need?

Once you have a sense of your spending priorities, you will want to determine how much income you will need when your paychecks cease. Only with a sense of a post-retirement budget will you know how much you must save. Financial advisers suggest you will need 70 percent to 80 percent of your working income, but you can live on less depending on your habits and priorities. Becky and I live as well as we ever did on 60 percent, and we could live on less without feeling deprived.

Often the largest category of expense within our monthly budget is "Unexpected and Irregular Expenses." Irregular expenses are those that, like insurance and taxes, don't appear every month. But they are predictable. "Unexpected" expenses actually are predictable; we just don't know when they will arise. You know you will have to replace an auto when repairs become more onerous than replacing the clunker. You don't know exactly when that will occur, but you can predict that eventually you will need newer wheels.

Not long ago, in the space of just three months, every major appliance (and many small appliances) in our home expired. I mean furnace, air conditioner, hot water heater, washer, dryer, dishwasher, refrigerator, attic fan, vacuum cleaner, computer, printer, stereo, video player, and two TVs. More recently we had to install two toilets and replace water-damaged floors and ceilings. None of the replacements gives us any more satisfaction than their predecessors. The timing of the joint demise of machines was a shock, but the *need* to replace them and make repairs soon was entirely predictable and budgetable, so we didn't panic or consider ourselves the victims of fate.

The following worksheet will help you determine how much money you will need to save to support a comfortable lifestyle after your working years. It works as well for younger men and women as for those much closer to retirement. An interactive version is available from the American Savings Education Council (ASEC) at http://www.asec.org/ballpark. ASEC president Don Blandin affirms that efforts at saving fail unless individuals and couples agree on their goal. Without a goal, "people save blindly and are constantly worried about whether they're going to make it or not."[2]

What Will You Need?

Planning for retirement is not a one-size-fits-all exercise. The purpose of the Ballpark Estimate, devised by the American Savings Education Council and available on its site (www.asec.org/ballpark), is simply to give you a basic idea of the savings you'll need when you retire.

If you are married, you and your spouse should each fill out your own Ballpark Estimate worksheet, taking your marital status into account when entering your Social Security benefit in number 2 below.

1. How much annual income will you want in retirement? (Figure at least 70 percent of your current annual income just to maintain your current standard of living. Really.) $ _____

2. Subtract the income you expect to receive annually from:
- **Social Security**
  If you make under $25,000, enter $8,000; between $25,000 and $40,000, enter $12,000; more than $40,000, enter $14,500. (For married couples: Lower-earning spouses should enter either their own benefit based on their income or 50 percent of the higher-earning spouse's benefit, whichever is higher.)

  For a more personalized estimate, enter the appropriate benefit figure from your Social Security statement from the Social Security Administration (you can ask for it by calling 800-772-1213, or online at www.ssa.gov). The Ballpark Estimate assumes you will begin receiving Social Security benefits at age 65; however, the age for full benefits is rising to 67. Your Social Security statement will provide a personalized benefit estimate based on your actual earning history. $ _____

- **Traditional Employer Pension**
  This is the kind of plan that pays a set dollar amount for life, where the dollar amount depends on salary and years of service (your employer can project this amount). – $ _____
- **Part-time income** – $ _____
- **Other** (an annuity, rental income, royalties, etc.) – $ _____

  This is how much you need to make up for each retirement year
  (Line 1 minus Line 2) $ _____

The gap will have to be filled out of your own savings, so to achieve the annual income you want you'll need a certain amount of money in the bank the day you retire. Accountants have devised a formula to determine just how much money you'll need. (The formula assumes a constant real rate of return of 3 percent after inflation, that you'll live to age 87 and that you'll begin to receive Social Security income at age 65. If you anticipate living longer than age 87 or earning less than a 3 percent real rate of return on your savings, you'll want to consider using a higher percentage of your current annual gross income as a goal on line 1.)

3. To determine the amount you'll need to save, multiply the amount you need to make up by the factor below. $ _____

Age at which you expect to retire: 55   Your factor is: 21.0
                                    60   18.9
                                    65   16.4
                                    70   13.6

4. If you expect to retire before age 65, multiply your Social Security benefit from line 2 by the factor below. + $ _____

Age at which you expect to retire: 55   Your factor is: 8.8
                                    60   4.7

5. Multiply your savings to date by the factor below (include money accumulated in a 401(k), IRA or similar retirement plan): – $ _____

If you want to retire in: 10 yrs. Your factor is: 1.3
                          15 yrs.   1.6
                          20 yrs.   1.8
                          25 yrs.   2.1
                          30 yrs.   2.4
                          35 yrs.   2.8
                          40 yrs.   3.3

Total additional savings needed at retirement
(Line 3 plus Line 4 minus Line 5): = $ _____

Don't panic. The accountants have devised another formula to show you how much to save each year in order to reach your goal amount. They factor in compounding of interest. That's where not only your money makes interest, but your interest starts earning interest as well, creating a snowball effect.

6. To determine the annual amount you'll need to save, multiply the total amount (from line 5) by the factor below. = $ _____

If you want to retire in: 10 yrs. Your factor is: 0.085
                          15 yrs.   0.052
                          20 yrs.   0.036
                          25 yrs.   0.027
                          30 yrs.   0.020
                          35 yrs.   0.016
                          40 yrs.   0.013

The Ballpark Estimate is designed to provide a rough estimate of what you will need to save annually to fund a comfortable retirement. It provides an approximation of projected Social Security benefits and utilizes only one of many possible rates of return on your savings. Ballpark reflects today's dollars and does not account for inflation; therefore, you should recalculate your savings needs on a regular basis and as your salary and circumstances change. You won't want to stop with the Ballpark Estimate; it is only a first step in the retirement planning process. You will need to do further analysis, either yourself using a more detailed worksheet or computer software, or with the assistance of a financial professional.

The joint EBRI and ASEC Web site (www.choosetosave.org) has more than one hundred financial calculators that can help you project living expenses, budget to save, calculate the advantages of credit card consolidation and many other aspects of financial planning.

In retirement you can count on some reduced expenses. For example, if you have a white-collar job now, your clothing budget will shrink later. And you will save on commuting costs, including lunches. If you are close to having your mortgage paid up, that will be a significant saving; but remember, if you have paid off your mortgage, you will still have to pay for taxes and insurance on your mortgage-free home. Until now, those expenses had been hidden in your monthly mortgage payment.

On the other hand, if you plan to travel and eat out often in retirement, those will be additional expenses. Once you lose employer-sponsored healthcare benefits, your medical expenses will rise as well. If you plan to move to another state where living expenses are lower, take into account the costs of selling your present home, the settlement costs for your retirement home, moving expenses, and the costs of furnishing your new home. You may decide to stay put. Retirement is not exile. Although many retirees eventually move into a smaller home or apartment, most choose to remain in the same community to be close to family, friends, and church.

The Cost of Enjoyment
The best things in life may not be completely free, but they needn't cost much. Most people gain their greatest enjoyment from friends, family, and conversation. If you enjoy reading or listening to music, the free public library is the place to haunt. It even offers free Internet access, so you're not required to have a computer at home once you're retired. Gardening and fishing involve some expense, but mostly labor.

In retirement you will have the time to indulge your pleasures, and time (until it runs out) is free. Senior citizen discounts apply to all kinds of entertainment, travel, and accommodations. Once you reach age fifty, you can join AARP for a pittance and discover the discounts and information to which you are entitled.

Even travel need not be expensive in retirement, unless you insist on a new car, an RV, or a boat. Becky and I use a British Airways VISA card for all our expenses. We are not frequent fliers, but every dollar we charge to the card for anything counts as a frequent flier mile. By charging every possible expense to the card we earn a free round-trip flight to Europe every year. Once we're at our destination, our vacations cost little more than if we had remained at home.

How can that be? The secret, as I explained in my book *Spiritual Simplicity*, is exchanging homes, our vacation practice for close to thirty years. When our daughters were still with us, we confined family vacations to the United States and Canada, enjoying quaint New England college towns; northern Maine; elegant Darien, Connecticut; oceanfront Wilmington, North Carolina; a mansion in Mississippi; and St. Catherine's in Ontario. Since Becky and I have been on our own, we have vacationed in Brigadoon-like villages in Scotland, thatched-roof cottages in England's Cotswolds and East Anglia, homes on the English Channel, and an island off Colchester, as well as Edinburgh, London, and Paris.

Once you arrive at your exchange destination, you enjoy all the comfort of someone else's home, kitchen, garden, books, stereo, and television, plus helpful neighbors. No cramped hotel rooms and expensive restaurants. No dirty laundry to drag back home either, because you have use of your hosts' washer and dryer. In Paris we shopped for fresh provisions daily in neighborhood markets. We prepared breakfast and dinner and packed a lunch for our day trips. Because we exchange not only homes but autos and pet care, the only cost is gas for our exchangers' car.

Don't assume you require an exceptional home or apartment in a trendy location to attract exchangers. We get frequent requests from people who have relatives living near us and want to pay them a visit without moving in on them. Even if you are single with a small apartment, take heart. You will find someone in a similar situation with whom to exchange. Contact HomeLink International at http://www.homelink.org to reach thousands of exchangers in many countries. If you are nervous about having strangers in your home, restrict your choices to experienced exchangers who can offer references, and arrange to meet them before you leave.

If Your Savings Fall Short

Rutgers University professor Barbara O'Neill helps people catch up on saving for retirement. If you are discouraged by the results of your "What Will You Need?" worksheet, consider six ways to increase your savings, as well as six strategies to reduce the amount of savings you will need. Stan Hinden, a retired *Washington Post* reporter, summarizes O'Neill's strategies.[3]

To increase your savings:

- Increase contributions to tax-deferred plans, such as a 401(k).
- Accelerate debt repayment so your monthly payments can be moved to retirement savings.
- Take a second job to earn additional income, which you can put into retirement savings.
- Invest more aggressively to achieve higher returns, but remember that a stock-heavy portfolio entails more risk.
- Invest strategically by choosing investments in mutual funds or in companies that will benefit by long-range demographic trends. Remember, though, that sector investing reduces diversification and increases potential for loss.
- Reduce taxes by investing in tax-free municipal bonds, putting money into a Roth IRA, or taking advantage of long-term capital gains tax rates.

To reduce the amount of savings needed for retirement:

- Trade down to a smaller home, which may lower your monthly expenses and give you a lump sum from the sale of your former home to put into your retirement account.
- Move to a less expensive community, which may reduce your cost of living, although it may put you far from family and friends.
- Delay retirement. A few extra years on the job can boost your retirement savings, pension, and Social Security benefits.
- Work after retirement from your primary job. With this added income, you can reduce the amount of money you have to withdraw from savings.
- Consider a reverse mortgage, which provides a monthly payment to homeowners and is repaid from the borrowers' equity when they sell the house or die.
- Make tax-efficient withdrawals from savings by taking money from taxable accounts first and tax-deferred accounts later.

Investing

Once you start saving, at whatever age, you are an investor—in yourself and in the rest of your life. That is, unless you're like my mother-in-law, who kept gold Krugerrands under the floorboards late in life, fearing that America was going the way of the Weimar Republic, when a loaf of bread cost a wheelbarrow of deutsche marks. Her savings were safe, but they didn't earn anything.

Andrew Tobias provides a handy formula for ensuring a nest egg when you reach retirement:

"Make a budget, scrimp and save, quit smoking, fully fund your retirement plan and start early—*tomorrow*—if you possibly can—putting away $100 or $500 or $5,000 a month, whatever you can comfortably afford, in two places: short- and intermediate-term Treasury securities, for money you may need in a few years; into no-load, low-expense stock market "index funds," both United States and foreign, for everything else. You will do better than 80 percent of your friends and neighbors."[4]

If you are under the age of fifty, experts suggest that you put 80 percent of savings into stock funds, 20 percent into bonds. As you approach retirement, move more into bonds for stability. Remember: you are not saving for a rainy day. Rather, you are investing in sunlight for the rest of your life.

If you find investing boring, you're like most people, including me. Happily, you don't have to do the work. The nation's mutual fund companies do it for us. Basically, they pool the savings of millions of Americans and invest for you, charging only a small service fee you will never miss. You deal with the funds entirely over the phone (they don't put you on "hold") and by mail or Internet. They regularly inform you how your money is doing. (If you're anxious, of course, you can check the newspaper every day, but I don't recommend it.)

Mutual funds are for people who don't intend to play the market, but only want to ensure a solvent future. Incidentally, your mutual fund savings aren't inaccessible. Just a phone call will return them to you in cash for any reason whatsoever, and you can transfer your savings from fund to fund just as easily. If your savings are in *tax-deferred* funds (like IRAs and 401(k)s) you will pay a penalty for early withdrawal.

A little consistent saving can make you a millionaire. Don't take my word for it. The magic is in compound interest. Say you're earning $35,000 and you put 4 percent of that in your employer's 401(k) retirement plan. That's just $27 each week out of your paycheck (less if you figure the taxes that would be assessed if you pocketed that $27). What's $27? The price of a book you could borrow instead from the library for free.

Assuming a 7 percent rate of return on your savings, you will have accumulated $590,134.11 in fifty years—or well over a million dollars if your employer matches your contributions. In fact, you may have much more, because over the long run stocks perform over 7 percent. But it's never too late to start.

To find mutual funds that appeal to you, consult the annual issues of *Money* and *Kiplingers* magazines that list the performance of all funds. They're in your public library. You'll see how much they have returned over the past one, five, and ten years. Despite some big winners, most funds don't perform as well as the market as a whole, so follow Andrew Tobias's advice and invest in "market index" funds that mimic the market as a whole. Of course, the market fluctuates daily, but you have a long time to live, and historically it rebounds and rises.

Spending

You are not saving for saving's sake, but to have money to spend to enjoy the rest of your life. Don't scrimp just to ensure that your children will have an inheritance. Teach them to be savers, too. Set priorities that satisfy your goals, not someone else's. Last year pet care was the third-largest expense in our family budget (after food and health expenses) because of our dog's and cats' serious health problems. We didn't mind. They are precious to us and give us joy.

Sometimes the cheaper or disposable products are the best, because they are less complicated. Our new heating and air conditioning system is only the budget model, admittedly less efficient than top-of-the-line units. But *Consumer Reports* warns that the more expensive systems need servicing more often at extra cost.

In my book *Spiritual Simplicity*, I outlined easy strategies for saving time and money, and even a few ways of making extra money. I won't repeat them here except to warn that any sensible budget and savings plan will founder if you allow big expenses to overwhelm you. Divorce, catastrophic illness, excessive college expenses, and major repair bills can spoil the glorious time you are saving for. Even when the economy was booming a few years ago, one of every seventy American families filed for bankruptcy every year.[5]

Although half of marriages end in divorce, most fail within the first five years, whereas divorce is relatively rare after retirement.[6] To forestall other financial tragedies, you can purchase life, health, disability, catastrophic illness, and long-term care insurance. You can even buy insurance that makes your mortgage payments if you lose your job. Some policies are rip-offs, and some are simply not worth the premiums. Remember, you are saving for enjoyment, not spending for security from setbacks.

Even though you will have a more modest budget in retirement, you will want to continue spending on others. Dickens's Ebenezer Scrooge learned the hard way that there's a difference between being frugal and being cheap. The former is a virtue, the latter a vice. Americans in general are frugal with themselves, shopping for quality and discounts. But they can be cheap with other people, leaving a tiny tip for good service instead of 15 percent or 20 percent. It's not wise to save at the expense of other people. They, too, need to support themselves.

Even in retirement one category in your budget should be devoted to saving the world, or at least a small part of it. It's up to you how you do it—through church or charities—but you must give something back as a token of gratitude for what you have been given. It's not really expensive to be generous. When author David Baldacci's first novel was a huge best-seller, he considered it unexpected good fortune and shared most of his royalties with his family and friends. With his second novel he became wealthy himself.

Ironically, the poorest one-fifth of Americans actually donate a larger percentage of their after-tax income to charity than Americans who earn $100,000 or more. Maybe that's because they know better what it's like to go without. Of course, wealthy people itemize their donations and get tax deductions. Still, on average, they contribute less than 3 percent of their income to making the world a better place.[7] People of faith recall Jesus's counsel: "Whatever you did for one of the least of these brothers of mine, you did for me" (Matthew 25:40). As you celebrate the rest of your life, you will have the leisure to volunteer your time and talent to organizations that help others. It's an inexpensive way of sharing some of the gold of your golden years.

Get Advice

There's wisdom in the cliché that one must sometimes spend money to make money. That's not an invitation to prepare for retirement at the gaming tables in Las Vegas or Atlantic City, but just a suggestion that you occasionally pay an expert for a little advice. If you are like most Americans, you already seek assistance with your income tax returns, but you may use a commercial tax preparer who learned the basics in a brief course and works only at filing time. Even certified public accountants (CPA) are hard-pressed at tax time to help you with your overall financial planning, but they are available at other times of the year to help you plan ahead.

A warning, though: don't ask anyone for financial advice who wants to sell you something. Some stockbrokers and insurance agents offer "free" financial planning that is biased. When Becky and I were approaching retirement, we went to a neighborhood CPA who had nothing to gain from her counseling but a $75 fee. For that, she told us everything we needed to protect our investments, reduce our taxes, and provide insurance against future disability. We've followed through on every one of her strategies.

One thing you and your spouse must each have is a will. How you distribute the wealth of your life testifies to the people and institutions you value. There is nothing more disheartening than to witness adult children and other prospective heirs fighting over their share of an estate. Assuming you have a will, it will probably need to be updated when you retire. And you will also want to file a "living will" if you don't want your life prolonged artificially and painfully during terminal illness. You should also draw up a separate document that indicates how your personal effects are to be distributed. Rest assured, it is not morbid to ask your adult children what they would like as personal keepsakes. Otherwise you risk having your possessions going to auction.

Americans move, on average, every five years. My parents' generation favored purchasing cemetery plots and headstones, and even prepaying funeral expenses, but that's because they were sure of the place they would always call home. If you are like most Americans, you are uncertain where you will end up, so such outlays may be premature. Still, you should make your wishes known. A wise and economical decision you can make now is to join your local nonprofit memorial society. Becky and I pay dues of just $5 a year to discover the competitive costs of dignified Christian burial or cremation in northern Virginia. Planning for the inevitable is not morbid, just farsighted and responsible.

For Poorer
Married couples exchange vows "for richer, for poorer" to affirm that love is of greater value than money in their lives together. However well you plan financially for the autumn and winter

of your lives, there is always the possibility that savings will run short and your standard of living will suffer, at least temporarily, if financial markets tumble.

It is wise to reflect that relative poverty is not necessarily an evil. In the Sermon on the Mount Jesus praised the poor. He pronounced them happy "for the kingdom of Heaven is theirs" (Matthew 5:3). Through the long centuries of Christian faith, voluntary poverty has been chosen by millions of faithful, who realized that one must empty oneself to give room for God to enter. Thoreau chose a life so simple that his neighbors called him poor. In point of fact, the very simplicity of his life left him free to enjoy it without fretting about money.

As Thomas Moore explains, "The truly wealthy person is the one who 'owns' it all—land, air, and sea. . . . The *experience* of wealth is, after all, subjective. For some, to be wealthy is to have credit cards paid off, for others it requires owning a Rolls Royce or two. . . . The problem lies not in having too much or too little, but in taking money literally, as a fetish rather than as a medium." He concludes: "The soul is nurtured by want as much as by plenty."[8] Still, want need not be cause for worry.

I mentioned earlier that only 15 percent of aging Americans can expect to be assisted financially by their families. The numbers would be far greater if aging parents told their adult children something about their needs and finances. AARP discovered recently that aging parents consider the discussion of money to be taboo within their families. The survey noted that three in ten adult children suspect their parents need help at some point but will not ask for it.[9]

Financial columnist Michelle Singletary was frustrated when she attempted to assist her aging grandmother: "It was incredibly difficult to raise the subject with Big Mama. She refused to get a will. She wouldn't even consider moving from her home even as her health disintegrated. Big Mama's idea of discussing her finances was pointing to a big beige purse she kept locked in her bedroom closet. 'Everything you need to know is right there in that purse,' she told me. 'You can look through it if I get sick or die.'"[10]

My mother, who outlived my father by a decade, was not unlike Big Mama in being secretive about her finances, which were modest. But she gave her lawyer a list of her assets, wrote a sound will, and gave him durable powers of attorney, so he could make decisions for her when she was incapacitated. Finally, she had her local bank trust department pay her bills and hold her assets. Unfortunately, she did not have a living will, so I had to persuade her doctor that she did not want to have her life prolonged artificially in her terminal illness. Fortunately, he took my word.

Planning ahead for life alone after the death of a spouse is even more critical and clearly involves more than finances.

Organizing Your Spending

I often ask Becky to remind me of things I need to do, but I can't rely on her for everything. The best kind of reminder is something visible that jogs one's memory. Pay as many bills as possible at the same time each month. If they're not due immediately, tape them to the proper mailing date in a desk calendar. In retirement, you will be required to pay estimated state and federal taxes four times a year and property taxes every six months. Remind yourself of the due dates by taping the envelopes in the proper place in your calendar.

Set aside a few hours at the end of each month to consult your checkbook to see where you stand financially. People of all ages quickly lose track of cash. Use a credit card whenever possible and you will have a record of your purchases. Pay off the full amount of the balance each billing cycle so you won't be burdened by interest payments. Buy staple foods and household items in bulk.

They won't cost nearly as much, and you will not have to remember to resupply so often. In every case, simplify your routines so there isn't as much to remember. Carry a pocket notebook or small recorder, and make notes as they occur to you.

Establish routines so they become unthinking habits. Pay bills and change the furnace filter the same day each month. Do the week's shopping on the same day of the week. Bank by mail or computer. Keep a supply of postage stamps. If you take medications every day, purchase a container that allows you to separate them by the day of the week, and leave that container where you will see it first thing in the morning and last thing at night. My parents always wrapped a rubber band around a finger to remind them of something that had to be done. It worked for them, never for me. Keep duplicate house and car keys, and hide a set in a magnetic holder on your car's frame. A lost key is not a tragedy if you have another at hand. Keep important papers either in a safe deposit box or in a fireproof safe at home. If you don't use much cash, you won't forget where you hid it. Make a list of your credit cards, and keep the list in your desk calendar should you lose a card.

The Price of Pleasure

It is possible to live beneath your means, but few Americans do, especially while they are still gainfully employed. But in our later years we will scrutinize our limited incomes and may become stingy with ourselves and those we love. Consider whether you are overspending on necessities when you could be devoting a larger portion of your dollars and time to enjoying a few luxuries.

At New York's Four Seasons Hotel the same bottle of Evian water costs $10 from room service and $1.50 from the nearest deli. With forethought you can do even better, turning mere water into sparkling wine! For example, if you elect to drink tap water instead of bottled water every day, you could purchase champagne every few weeks with your savings. Whatever your tastes, budget to invest in real enjoyment.

I will skip my sermon that the best things in life are free in favor of arguing that enjoyment need not be expensive. Much of luxury is only for display, and the rich are notoriously wasteful with their pleasures. During America's Gilded Age, the hosts of a famous New York party in 1897 proudly announced that it cost them $370,000 (millions in today's dollars). One guest, August Belmont, came to the party in a $10,000 suit of gold-inlaid armor, which he discarded before the evening was out. No one is around to wax nostalgic about the fun Belmont and company had at such expense.[11]

Elegance has no price tag. When the impoverished Audrey Hepburn moved with her mother from war-torn Belgium to London to study dance, her entire wardrobe consisted of a black blouse, skirt, slacks, and slippers. Nevertheless, her classmates considered her the most elegantly dressed student. Her secret: wearing a different brightly colored scarf each day.[12]

Of course, those who transform the ordinary into the elegant sometimes charge outrageously for the pleasure. Christian Delouvrier, the soft-spoken chef of New York's exclusive restaurant, Lespinasse, defends the $35 price of a bowl of leek and potato soup because it contains truffles. "I pay $1,600 a pound for my Italian truffles," he argues. "You can pay less, of course, but then they would not be as good. Without the truffles, the soup would probably cost maybe $10 or $12."[13] I must confess that leek and potato soup is my favorite, and that Becky makes it in great freezable batches (albeit without truffles) for pennies. Elegant but affordable luxuries can get to be a handsome habit now that you have the time to savor them. Rest assured, you will not shrink spiritually as you enjoy your life more.

5. In Sickness and in Health:

Live Long and Prosper

The wish to be well is a part of becoming well.
—Seneca, "Epistles"

Dear Friend, I pray that you may enjoy good health and that all may go well with you, even as your soul is getting along well.
—3 John 1:2

The Nicene Creed asserts our faith in bodily resurrection, which suggests that we ought to take good care of our physical selves this side of eternity. Although Americans spend more per person on health care than the citizens of any other nation, the investment has not ensured a higher quality of life for us.

God designed the human animal to last more than a hundred years, but most of us manage to survive only a fraction of that span. The problem with prematurely deceased people, as with short-lived automobiles, is poor maintenance. By our habits we consign our-selves to the human junkyard. Few of us will live long enough to die of old age.

Fortunately, religious faith teaches respect for our physical selves. More than two-hundred fifty studies have demonstrated that men and women who employ religious or spiritual practices in their lives will, on average, live longer, be ill less regularly, and be less *prone to cancer than nonbelievers. As we prepare to celebrate the rest of our lives we are ill-advised to rely on miracles. Our health is our own responsibility.*

When his first Model Ts were abandoned by their owners to auto graveyards, Henry Ford sent teams of his engineers to determine why the autos had expired. The experts discovered that the machines had not died of old age; rather, only one essential part had failed, rendering the whole vehicle useless. With that information, Ford ordered his technicians to design automobiles in which *all* their parts would wear out at about the same time. To our knowledge, the automaker was not being cynical, just cost-effective.

All men and women develop some physical ailments before retirement, but as we age we are more aware of our mortality. Unlike unthinking automobiles, we can maintain our health, lengthen our lives, and even enhance our sense of well-being. Remember, our bodies are the temples of our souls. We need to keep our temple in good repair.

Becky and I are both fortunate to have a physician who sees us routinely four times a year, insists on annual physical examinations, and is quick to send us for tests and to specialists. He keeps up on his medical literature and is a devotee of diet and exercise. He considers ill health to be a personal affront. If he could manage, he would keep us alive forever. His mantra is that his patients' health and well-being are ultimately in their hands, not his, but he finds most of his patients to be careless about caring for themselves.

A Rude Awakening

It wasn't until I turned fifty that I was shocked into taking my doctor's advice. My wake-up call came as I stood on a subway platform at evening rush hour in Washington, D.C. A chronic insomniac, I was at the time so sleep-deprived that I ached from head to foot. It took immense effort in my stressful job to focus my attention and get from task to task and moment to moment.

In my family life I was a short-tempered zombie. Moreover, I had become increasingly prone to infection. In the previous year I had suffered two serious bouts of pneumonia plus strep throat. Standing there on the platform wallowing in self-pity, I looked down at the subway rails and realized for the first time why some people prefer oblivion to the lives they lead.

As I entertained that morbid thought, a stranger standing next to me on the crowded platform keeled over and fell onto the tracks below. Shocked out of my reverie, I jumped down and dragged her unconscious body from the rails. Other commuters reached down from the platform and pulled her limp body back before the next train arrived, lifting me to safety as well. Hers was clearly not a suicide attempt, but a near-tragic fainting. All I could conclude was that if a professional woman still in her twenties could place herself in such danger, a half-century-old man had better start looking after his own life.

Today, having turned seventy, I am healthier than I was in my thirties, less prone even to common colds. I have a lengthy litany of medical conditions, some serious, none of which has been *cured*. Yet all are neutralized due to healthier habits, diet, and medication, and I even feel better than I did when just half my present age. I credit my doctor and my wife, each of whom reminds me that I am not just a thinking machine, but a complete creature consisting of body, spirit, and emotions. They have taught me that good health and longevity require tending to all three.

The late presidential candidate Adlai Stevenson was fond of quoting this conversation between an aunt and her favorite niece:

Aunt to niece: "What do you want to be when you grow up?"

Niece: "Alive."[1]

Wouldn't we all? Dr. Walter M. Boritz II of Stanford University Medical School insists that the human animal is designed to last over a hundred years, but most of us manage to survive only a fraction of that span.[2] Unfortunately, our Creator did not provide us with extended warranties. The problem with death-prone people, as with short-lived automobiles, is poor maintenance. By our habits we consign ourselves too soon to the human junkyard. Few of us live long enough to die of old age. Our doctors are not to blame. Most of us die of self-administered abuse and indifference. Of course, tragically, some persons who do everything right are stricken with disease.

Living Long and Well

A strong case can be made that modern medicine has already provided us with the opportunity to live long and well. Life expectancy has risen by more than 50 percent since 1920, and infant mortality has plummeted 2000 percent since the turn of the twentieth century.[3] Infectious diseases have been largely controlled by a combination of public sanitation, antibiotics, and inoculations. Heart surgery and organ transplants have literally given millions a new lease on life. Stem cell and genetic research promise to make it possible to replace or restore malfunctioning organs, perhaps in our lifetime.

At the dawn of the new century, a group of 150 scientists interviewed by Michio Kaky of the City University of New York predicted that, if new technologies are made widely available, a child born today can expect to live 130 years.[4] You and I are not likely to thrive to that advanced age, but we have available to us a widening array of opportunities to ensure a long, vigorous, and relatively pain-free life.

It all starts with your determination to look after your health, then with finding a dependable doctor who is interested in your total well-being, not just the symptoms you complained about during your last visit. Finally, it's a matter of nutrition, exercise, sufficient rest, and a positive attitude—all those things our mothers nagged us about when we were children. Now we must nag ourselves.

There are two basic myths about staying healthy as we age. "And they're both baloney," says Carol Colleran of Florida's Hanley-Hazelden Center. "The first misconception is that it really doesn't make any difference if you change after twenty or thirty years, because you've already done all the damage you can do (to yourself). And the second myth is the moldy one that says you can't teach an old dog new tricks."[5]

Our passionate hearts, the poet Yeats lamented, are fastened to a dying animal. He was wrong in this respect: we are not dead until we stop functioning altogether; until then we can be fully alive. Fully two-thirds of physical ailments and premature deaths are caused by bad lifestyle and can be prevented by adopting good habits no matter how late in life we start.[6]

Prayer, Joy, and Positive Thinking

Happy people live longer. So do people with religious beliefs and positive attitudes—whereas negative thinking is a kind of suicide. Doctors in Finland discovered that people who consider themselves unhealthy die at an earlier age.[7] Social epidemiologist Jeff Levin, summarizing many studies, reports that religious people live, on average, seven years longer than other Americans.[8] Johns Hopkins University researchers note that attending a religious service at least once a month more than halves the risk of dying of heart disease, emphysema, suicide, and some forms of cancer.[9]

It also helps to have others pray for you. A 1988 study by cardiologist Randolph Byrd confirmed that coronary care patients prayed for by strangers enjoyed a significantly higher recovery rate than those not prayed for. A decade later another study confirmed Byrd's results and prompted a large-scale study at Harvard Medical School.[10]

Is this a miracle? Not necessarily. Levin argues that religious people embrace more temperate, less risky, and much healthier lifestyles because they feel responsible to their Creator for maintaining their physical and mental well-being. Such a lifestyle promotes a hopeful, contented, and less stressful outlook, which is health-enhancing. Church membership also offers social interaction and mutual support, which "seem to buffer or mitigate the negative effects of stress on health."[11] The AARP reports that adult children aged forty-five to fifty-five who care for their own aging relatives put prayer and faith ahead of doctors, friends, and institutions as their greatest comfort.[12] That comfort clearly rubs off on those they care for.

To *stay* well during the rest of your life, you must be like your own physician, dispensing prescriptions that include sleep, diet, and exercise, along with positive thinking, steady breathing, proper posture, a calm mind, and frequent laughter. Contentment is good medicine. So is laughter. Joy is even better. Love is the very best nostrum. If you have your health, you may not have *everything*, but you will have a foundation on which to support the best years of your life.

Wellness

There's more to good health than popping pills. Wellness is not just the absence of illness but the positive pursuit of contentment and vitality. A Gallup poll reveals that 85 percent of Americans acknowledge that their physical well-being depends on how well they take care of themselves.[13] Ironically, medical science looks at life through the wrong end of the telescope, focusing on disease and dysfunction. By contrast, health maintenance concentrates on wellness of body, mind, and spirit.

In 1984 author Greg Anderson was diagnosed with metastatic cancer and told he had thirty days to live. Conventional medicine gave up on him. Rallying to his own aid, he soon became cancer-free. His harrowing experience prompted him to create the Wellness Institute, which is dedicated to helping people become responsible for their own well-being. If his "22 Laws of Wellness" strike you as clichéd, reflect that nuggets of wisdom achieve the status of clichés because they are true. Here is my synopsis of Anderson's credo:

1. Life's joy, not its length, is the measure of wellness.
2. We are in charge of our wellness.
3. Wellness demands health of body, mind, and spirit.
4. To be well, keep physically and mentally active.
5. Eat for nourishment and enjoyment, not compensation.
6. When ill, seek the least-invasive medical treatment.
7. Stress aggravates illness, so control your response to your symptoms.
8. Acknowledge your emotions, but don't get stuck with negative ones.
9. You already have everything in your life to be happy.
10. Respect human dignity in yourself and in all others.
11. Deal with others in such a way that no one loses and everyone wins.
12. Abandon regret for the past and anxiety about the future. Live the present moment.

13. Focus on life as a journey rather than a destination. Don't keep asking yourself, "Am I there yet?"
14. Don't lurch into life, but act calmly from wisdom.
15. Pursue personal growth, not the Fountain of Youth.
16. Find a purpose in life and devote yourself to it as your personal mission.
17. By helping others, you help yourself.
18. Consider everything you have as a gift for which you alone are responsible.
19. Forgive others, then forgive yourself.
20. Be grateful for all the things that are going well for you.
21. Make peace with yourself.
22. Love unconditionally.[14]

The Problem of Pain

Many of the books in the Bible provide a gritty portrayal of human life. Beginning with the account of Adam and Eve in Eden, the Bible reveals that God has our best interests at heart, but that people often make life worse for themselves. As C. S. Lewis acknowledged, "All people, whether Christian or not, must be prepared to live a life of discomfort. The possibility of pain is inherent in the very existence of the world where souls can meet. When souls become wicked they will certainly use this possibility to hurt one another; and this, perhaps, accounts for four-fifths of the sufferings of men."[15]

Moreover, many of the pains and discomforts we associate with old age can be traced to bad habits indulged in our youth or to accidents that could have been avoided. Still, it is wise to remember that pain is sometimes chosen to achieve a better good. The soldier endangers his life for the sake of others. God, in the person of his Son, elected to suffer and die for love.

Physical pain is intended to be a warning of some physical dysfunction we must set right. It is good that a toothache drives us to the dentist. Physical discomfort is a reminder that redemption requires our cooperation. As Lewis noted, "The settled happiness and security which we all desire, God withholds from us by the very nature of the world: but joy, pleasure, and merriment he has scattered broadcast: The security we crave would teach us to rest our hearts in this world and oppose an obstacle to our return to God. . . . Our Father refreshes us on the journey with some pleasant inns, but will not encourage us to mistake them for home."[16]

When Vincent Price's wife died after a protracted illness, the actor demanded of a priest why God would allow such a painful end to her life. The priest's answer is not revealed in Price's biography, but it was clearly inadequate to dispel his grief, prompting him to leave the practice of his religious faith.

I am often asked how to console a person who has suffered loss or painful illness. I answer that God chose in love to suffer and die for God's creatures rather than work an easy miracle. Accordingly, we cannot expect a reprieve from the painful facts of life that he did not offer to himself.

Revealingly, people who suffer fire, floods, drought, and other violent acts of nature seldom blame God for their loss. Rather, they typically exclaim, "Thank God, it could have been worse," and get back to making things better. Pain and the aging process are equally natural. In the Bible, Job's sufferings and loss were unmerited, but so too were his previous and subsequent health and wealth, let alone his very existence. They are all gifts, and fragile ones at that. To embrace later life "for better, for worse" is to accept that the suffering God *allows* among us but does not *cause*. Indeed, on the cross, his Son accepted it himself.

Pain, Pain, Go Away

Biotechnologists predict that in the next century men and women will live indefinitely long lives, dying mainly from accidents, violence, and neglect—not from disease or old age. Humans will be like classic automobiles, kept going with spare parts and periodic overhauls. Regular injections of stem cells will revitalize human organs. But there will still be pain.

Pain, of course, is not itself an illness but only a sign of something gone wrong. Unfortunately, pain *shouts* when a whisper would suffice to remind us to seek a remedy for the underlying malady. As we age, most of us can be reconciled to non-fatal chronic conditions, but not to the pain that accompanies them. So we need to locate ways to neutralize the agony that goes with illness.

Fortunately, since pain is subjective, it can be managed through our reaction to it. Unfortunately, many doctors expect "good" patients not to complain of pain, but to grin and bear it. If that is your doctor's attitude, don't buy into it. Everyone is subject to illness from time to time, but no one need be victimized by pain. New drug-delivery systems allow pain-relieving remedies to be absorbed at constant levels without side effects such as drowsiness and nausea. Transdermal patches, nasal sprays, and tiny electronic devices allow pain-relievers to seep through the skin. Moreover, some new pills apply steady medication for twelve hours.

Pain can be literally crippling, so don't hesitate to ask your doctor to prescribe something effective. Medical schools still provide scant training in pain management, and many physicians persist in dismissing chiropractors as quacks. Many doctors hesitate to prescribe narcotics even to terminally ill patients for fear that they will create addiction, hasten death, or involve them in malpractice suits. Dr. B. Eliot Cole of the American Academy of Pain Management protests that "a patient who wants to commit suicide to get relief from pain is not receiving the kind of care he or she needs. That care is available—patients and their families need to demand it."[17]

Mind Over Matter

The young T. E. Lawrence (of Arabia) made a display of his grit by letting matches burn down to his fingertips, and displaying no reaction to the pain. When others tried to duplicate his skill, screaming in agony, they asked him for his secret. The trick, he revealed, is not to *mind* the pain.

Like yogis who walk on burning coals, Lawrence was on to something. Franz Alexander, MD, notes that "the most fundamental fact which we know about the process of life . . . in spite of its neglect by biology and medicine . . . [is] the fact that the mind rules the body."[18] As we age, we can control our reaction to pain, making it tolerable and keeping it from compromising the quality of our lives.

Pain is often aggravated by tension, anxiety, and physical deterioration. By neutralizing those aggravations, suffering is eased. To that end, pain clinics prescribe changes in diet and environment, and promote relaxation techniques, exercise programs, and antidepressants. When we are relaxed, fit, and in tolerably good spirits, we can cope with even chronic pain.

Because athletes are naturally competitive, they play *through* their pain, treating illness as just another opponent to be challenged and beaten. At the age of forty-nine, Olympic gold medal skater Peggy Fleming developed breast cancer. Two days after the operation she was out running and soon resumed lifting weights. Shelley Hamlin, former president of the Ladies Professional Golf Association, had her left breast removed in a modified radical mastectomy. Less than seven months later she returned to the tour and won her first LPGA event. Arnold Palmer at age sixty-seven had his cancerous prostate removed and was back on the course in eight weeks. Athletes insist on being fit and active even after painful surgery. If need be, so can we.

A positive attitude is our first line of defense. It starts with gratitude for life itself. Author John Robert McFarland refused to allow cancer to make him its victim: "I'm so grateful I never have bad days. I have nauseated days and frightened days. Tired days and hurting days. Long days and short days. Silent days and alone days. Mouth-sore days and swollen hands days. Cold days and warm days. But no bad days. I'm so grateful."[19]

Novelist and TV writer D. Keith Mano has Parkinson's disease. He insists that it is only a "condition" rather than an affliction, and treats it the way a child would an imaginary friend—as a constant companion, someone to talk to and argue with. He even has a name for his companion—Bert. A condition is company, Mano says: "Its habits may seem uncouth, but at least you're never alone."

Now on the drug Sinemet, Mano suffers fewer Parkinson's symptoms, but he acknowledges that the drug is effective for only three to five years, and it has side-effects. He reveals that "something in me still needs the hallowing of my condition—the coping and the heightened awareness. The difficulty. Would I like to be cured? Sure. But there are aspects of Bert I would miss. We have been strangely intimate."[20]

Confronting Pain with Guided Imagery

Everyone's pain is personal. Anyone who says "I feel your pain" is fooling you. Because suffering is subjective, we tend to be inarticulate in describing it. Accordingly, physicians have difficulty locating and relieving it. Local anesthetics commonly used for minor operations enjoy only brief effectiveness. Aspirin and other common pain remedies medicate the entire body rather than the site of pain and can cause unpleasant side effects. Sometimes the "cure" can seem worse than the illness. Experts in pain control suggest the first step in relieving pain is to *confront* it by describing it to ourselves. All pain is not alike. Once you meet the pain and define it you can be on your way to mastering it. For example, an arthritis sufferer knows that inflammation of her joints is the cause of her agony. That knowledge allows her to objectify it, developing its image in her mind. One patient pictured herself as the "Tin Lady," like the Tin Man in *The Wizard of Oz*. When pain struck, she imagined squirting lubricant on her agony, just as Dorothy applied oil to the Tin Man's squeaky joints.

The trick here is to separate oneself from the pain. Instead of complaining "*I* hurt," you declare, "The pain is *there*." Once you localize your pain, you can step back from it and deal with it. A patient suffering from Reynaud's syndrome, a malady that causes painfully cold hands and feet, is helped by knowing that his problem stems from poor circulation. With that knowledge he can help himself by imagining hot compresses wrapped around his feet and thick woolen mittens on his hands.

To be sure, the aim of imaging pain is not to fool yourself but to separate yourself from the pain—and the technique works. As soon as you can picture the pain as tangible, you can ease it from your body by auto-suggestion. By picturing warmth, you can bring warmth to your extremities. By relaxing, you can feel the pain seep from your body. Here are the steps in guided imagery for pain control:

1. Discover what your pain feels like.
2. Create a vivid image of your pain.
3. Find an image of pain relief (e.g., "oiling" the Tin Man).
4. Begin relaxing with slow, steady breathing.
5. Detach your mind from the weight of your body.

6. Concentrate on the image of your pain.

7. Imagine your pain draining away.

Obviously, this regimen takes more time and effort than swallowing a pain pill, but it can become second nature, engaging the "placebo effect" in your favor. It's well known that many people get well because they *expect* medication to work. Substitute a sugar pill for the real thing, and many will still improve. With guided imagery you can make your expectations do the work.

Confronting Depression

Clinical depression is a special kind of suffering that disproportionately afflicts many men and women in their later years. Nearly one-sixth of Americans over the age of sixty-five find themselves overwhelmed by a sad, anxious mood that persists for lengthy periods, aggravated by loss of interest or pleasure in activities they once enjoyed.[21] Other symptoms include:

- Feelings of worthlessness, hopelessness, and guilt
- Difficulty in concentrating and making decisions
- Insomnia or oversleeping
- Appetite and weight loss
- Fatigue and loss of energy
- Agitation, restlessness, and irritability
- Frequent thoughts of death or suicide

Clinical depression is not a normal part of aging, nor is it just temporary sadness, disappointment, or discouragement. The exact cause of the disease is unknown but assumed to be a combination of biological and social factors. Research suggests that it may be related to an imbalance in serotonin, a natural substance that acts as a messenger between nerve cells in the brain. Depression afflicts men and women of all ages but is probably more prevalent among seniors because many sense a loss of control over their lives as they age (something this book is meant to remedy).

Once diagnosed, depression is successfully treated by a combination of psychotherapy and antidepressant medication, typically SSRIs (selective serotonin reuptake inhibitors) that help restore serotonin balance in the brain. The purpose of talk therapy is to reverse negative and even morbid thinking that can become ingrained as a habit among depressed people.

But most of us are subject to the blues. We must rouse ourselves and cure ourselves. I do not mean to minimize the blues. I am subject to them myself. Usually they stem from protracted (but not fatal) illness, disappointment, or discouragement. Whatever their cause, they drive the affected person further into himself or herself, when the only permanent relief is to break out of the misery. If you feel cooped up, you must get out. If you have no friends to talk to, find a support group in your church or community. If you find it harder to manage the usual routines of living, you must simplify those tasks. In short, we must change the conditions that are responsible for our feeling bad.

Sleep

The three pillars of personal health management are sleep, exercise, and nutrition. In retirement you will have the time and leisure to pay attention to all three.

By rights, sleep should be the easiest, because it literally involves doing *nothing*. Moreover, in retirement you no longer have to set the alarm clock for the crack of dawn as you did before. But you need *enough* sleep at any age. If you are tired and inattentive during the day, you cannot enjoy yourself. You are probably not getting enough sleep.

The best regimen at any age is to maintain the same hours for retiring and waking every day of the week. Naps are one of the pleasant dividends of senior life, but they don't compensate for inadequate rest at night. If you are like me (and one-third of your fellow Americans), you have trouble sleeping well consistently. If poor rest is seriously interfering with your waking hours, sleep clinics can reveal the causes. Often the culprit is troubled breathing, or apnea. Snoring is not simply a trial for your bedmate but can be dangerous to your health.

Dr. James W. Pearce, director of the Sleep Disorders Center of the Pacific in Honolulu, admits that even he misses sleep occasionally and gets a truly refreshing night's rest only on vacation. Here are some of his tips for the remainder of the year:

1. Don't oversleep because of the previous night's wakefulness.
2. If you can't sleep, stop trying. Sleep can't be forced.
3. Have a light snack before bedtime.
4. Don't take drugs, including nicotine, alcohol, and caffeine. Even antihistamines before bedtime can have irritating side effects.
5. Practice relaxation techniques, with the help of a pre-recorded audiotape if necessary.
6. Don't worry if you don't get eight hours. You may not need that much rest.
7. Exercise earlier in the day, not before bedtime.
8. Use the bedroom for sleep and sex, nothing else (not eating, TV watching, reading, or working). In fact, if sex stimulates you (instead of relaxing you) move your love life to a different room and time.
9. If you can't get to sleep until 3:00 AM but must wake at 7:00 AM, go to bed at 3:00 AM. After a week of sleeping well for four hours a night, retire fifteen minutes earlier the next night and work your way incrementally to a full night's sleep.[22]

You might consider Ben Franklin's cure for insomnia, which my wife swears by. In winter, Ben turned down the bedclothes so both sheets absorbed the chill of the room, doffed his nightshirt, and walked around the bedroom until he was uncomfortably cold. Thereupon he returned to bed and tucked himself in, gradually feeling warmth return. The regimen, he attested, converted his bed from an enemy of sleep into a friend.

In my own battles with insomnia, I tried both over-the-counter and prescription nostrums for sleep. The former make you feel drugged the next morning. The latter may induce amnesia and personality change and become habit-forming. I was prescribed the drug Halcion when it was a state-of-the-art remedy. As I mentioned earlier, it turned me into a cantankerous Mr. Hyde before I fell asleep. When I awoke, my family told me what a horror I had been, but I had no recollection of it. Because of similar reports, Halcion was banned in Great Britain.

Exercise

Just because exercise is currently fashionable doesn't mean it is popular. Despite Nike's urging the population to "just do it," only one-third of us do.[23] As we age we are more inclined to become sedentary. Part of the appeal of exercise is that it enhances our feeling of well-being, but today it is also used as part of a regimen to keep weight down and make people feel more attractive. But its real importance is to keep us healthy as we age. Ironically, as our lives become more stressful, we neglect stress-reducing exercise—a life-shortening combination. Darwin was right about the survival of the fittest. Don't expect your doctor to tell you how to exercise. Most physicians were never taught about physical fitness in medical school, and exercise is not mentioned in many of the leading medical textbooks even today.

The first time I ever heard the word exercise from my doctor was when I developed high blood pressure in middle age, then again when I was tested as a borderline diabetic. Still, it's never too late to start. The benefits of exercise for longevity are proven. In 1986 the *Journal of the American Medical Association* reported that for every hour spent exercising, two to three hours of life are gained. The benefits are most apparent after the age of seventy.[24] The positive effect of exercise on mood and mental health is almost immediate.

Even changing just one habit for the better can make a huge difference. The Cooper Institute in Dallas discovered that overweight men who stayed fit were two-thirds less likely to die prematurely of heart disease than overweight men who did not exercise.[25] A change of habit can also improve your sex life. A Harvard School of Public Health study discovered that older men who exercise twenty to thirty minutes a day are only half as likely to suffer impotence than their sedentary brothers.[26]

The real purpose of exercise is cardiovascular conditioning. The heart, lungs, blood vessels, tendons, and bones are brought to their highest working efficiency. We make better use of oxygen, make the best use of food, and even eliminate body wastes more effectively. This requires endurance (or aerobic) exercise, not just techniques for stretching and firming and sculpting your body. Three sessions a week of sustained, moderately vigorous exercise for thirty minutes is adequate. Before vigorous exercise you must loosen up so you won't strain tight muscles, but doctors are less certain about the benefits of stretching. In aerobic exercise you will break into a sweat.

No equipment is needed. Fast walking will do the trick. So will swimming if a pool is handy. Researchers suspect the three-times-a-week optimal exercise regimen has roots in our primitive makeup. Eskimos and other hunter-gatherer populations chase their prey three times a week, resting on alternate days.

Textbooks tell us that for best results we should exercise at 70 percent of our maximum. That means determining your pulse rate. For a sixty-year-old the 70 percent level should be something like 112 beats per minute; for a seventy-five-year-old, 101 beats.

In addition to cardiovascular conditioning, muscle-building exercise can be important. Women run the risk of developing osteoporosis after menopause. Strength training can help retain muscle mass and bone density.

Nutrition

The words nutrition and diet are often used interchangeably, but increasingly diet describes weight-loss regimens. As we age we tend to gain weight. Perhaps you need to lose weight to be healthy.

As a child I observed meatless Fridays and occasional days of fast and abstinence with my parents. Jews have dietary restrictions, and Muslims prescribe fasts as well. Their purpose is to make believers think of food (and life itself) as a gift, not a given. In a secular fast-food, snack-food culture, where we eat on the run, we are not only inclined to be thoughtless about food but fail to enjoy it sufficiently.

Eating is a pleasure. Arguably, it is the most reliable and democratic of pleasures, and the one most open to variety. Sex may be orgasmic, but cuisine can be an art and is a renewable feast. If you doubt me, check any bookstore and count the titles devoted to food and drink. There are more cookbooks in print than books devoted to pleasing all our other senses combined.

Eating sensibly does not mean denying oneself the pleasure of the palate. I was brought up with Popeye cartoons promoting the nutritional advantages of spinach. I loathed canned spinach, but as an adult discovered fresh spinach. Now, on the annual occasion when Becky and I splurge on a dinner at the Savoy Grill in London, I request creamed spinach even though it is not on the menu.

Food manufacturers now cater to good nutrition with tasty, low-salt, low-cholesterol, low-carbohydrate, and sugar-free versions of their regular products. But they can't force us to eat them. The late Dr. John Knowles, administrator of Massachusetts General Hospital and president of the Rockefeller Foundation, insisted that "over 99 percent of us are born healthy and are made sick as a result of personal misbehaviors and environmental conditions."[27] We can easily control something as enjoyable as our nutrition.

Diet gurus have conflicting thoughts about optimal nutrition, but they agree on these guidelines endorsed by the National Academy of Sciences:

1. Reduce your consumption of saturated and unsaturated fats to 30 percent of total calories. This is easily accomplished by trimming excess fat from meat; avoiding fried foods; and cutting back on butter, cream, and salad dressing—or switching to the low-fat or no-fat versions.
2. Increase your consumption of fresh fruit and vegetables and whole-grain cereals. These contain nutrients and fiber that protect against cancer and other diseases.
3. Eat salt-cured and charcoal-broiled foods only on rare occasions.
4. Drink alcoholic beverages in moderation.

In addition, the late health researcher Nathan Pritkin advised *eliminating* the following altogether from the diet:

1. All added salt
2. All beverages containing caffeine

3. *Refined* sugar and flour
4. Pepper and hot spices
5. Hydrogenated fats
6. Food containing artificial additives and preservatives

Bon appetit!

Dealing with Doctors

Becky's and my internist routinely runs an hour late on his appointments. We've learned not to mind his tardiness, because he spends as much time with each patient as that person needs. He treats people, not ailments. Despite disincentives from the HMOs that insure his patients' health care (and provide him a living), he regularly refers them to specialists for additional tests, as needed, and he encourages annual physicals, flu and pneumonia shots, exercise, and diet regimens.

I trust you will find such a doctor to work with you, but I must admit that it took many years and much dissatisfaction before we found him. Despite his professionalism, his practice cannot be very satisfying to him, because he rarely cures anyone, but can only diagnose illnesses, prescribe for his patients, and counsel them. Despite his effort to get people to take charge of their own health management, his waiting room is filled week after week with the same people, who expect him to work some miracle in bodies they have abused over the years.

Dr. Salvatore Scialla of Scranton, Pennsylvania, says, "I see my relationship with my patient as a marriage."[28] That's probably too much to ask of your doctor, but it must be a lasting relationship, and a democratic one at that, because you are jointly responsible for your health.

Best-selling author Dr. Bernie Siegel alarmingly reveals that many doctors care inadequately for their own well-being, so you may have to prod them to pay full attention to yours. On average, physicians have more problems abusing drugs and alcohol than their patients, as well as a higher suicide rate. And they die sooner than the rest of us after the age of sixty-five.[29]

Just because you are your doctor's patient doesn't mean that *patience* is the virtue you bring to that relationship. Dr. Bernie Siegel, who assists men and women stricken with cancer, reckons that 60 to 70 percent of patients are like actors auditioning for a part. They act the way they believe their doctor has scripted their role—passively taking their medicine, letting the physician do all the work, only balking when the doctor suggests that they make radical improvements in their lifestyles.

Another 10 to 15 percent of patients actually *welcome* serious illness (consciously or unconsciously) as a way of escaping their everyday problems. They do not seriously wish to be cured, so they fail to hold up their end of the doctor-patient relationship.

At the opposite extreme are 15 to 20 percent who refuse to play the victim. They choose to take charge of their health rather than expect the doctor to *make* them well. They question every procedure and dig in their heels until they are satisfied that it makes sense. They read everything they can about their condition so they can have an intelligent conversation with their doctor, and they are quick to demand second opinions.

Physicians have slowly come to acknowledge that the patients they consider feisty and uncooperative are the ones determined to get well, and who do improve. In a London sample, cancer patients with a "fighting spirit" enjoyed a ten-year survival rate of 75 percent, compared with only 22 percent for those who felt hopeless and helpless, and passively accepted whatever the doctors did for them.[30]

Preparing Yourself

Before you can collaborate effectively with your doctor to handle a medical condition, you need to ask yourself four questions:

1. *Do I want to live to be a hundred?* When gerontologist Ken Dychtwald asked hundreds of people this question, many answered that they didn't want to live much beyond retirement age, because they assumed that later life would be robbed of play, sex, and independence, and fraught with physical and financial problems. They were singing "The September Song" while still in the summer of their lives! Revealingly, patients long since retired answered differently. They wanted even *more* years. If you feel in control of your life and are willing to absorb the inevitable bumps and bruises, you will want to live longer, and you *will* live longer.

2. *What was going on in my life in the year or two before I became ill?* A condition you develop may be the by-product of some setback in your life to which you are not reconciled. If you face it, you may heal yourself.

3. *What does my condition mean to me?* Does it mean death or disability, or do you accept it as a life challenge? Dr. Siegel reports that one of his patients, on being told she had cancer, immediately donated her clothes to charity. She was burning her bridges after her and sealing her doom.

4. *Why do I need my illness?* Health conditions can serve purposes that have nothing to do with health. A serious illness in later life can be just an excuse to say no to the demands of other people. Perversely, being ill can make us feel important. How often have you heard older people boast about their ailments? Much oftener, I suspect, than you have heard people brag about how good they feel.[31]

A century ago, America's founding psychologist, William James, wrote, "The greatest discovery of my generation is that human beings, by changing the inner attitudes of their minds, can change the outer aspects of their lives."[32]

So can we all. Live long and prosper!

Never Too Late to Live Better

Becky and I are accustomed to buying our cars used, then driving them until they're about to expire. We used to hand them down to our daughters when the girls couldn't afford anything better. Now, as adults, they politely decline our clunkers.

By swapping homes with couples in England, Scotland, and France every summer, Becky and I enjoy practically expense-free summer vacations. But we have to exchange cars with our exchangers as well, which means we must leave something reliable for them to drive. By 1995, our 1982 station wagon was long past the prime of its life, so we ventured out to replace it with another sensible wagon not so old.

To make a long story short, we came back from the used car lot the owners of a magnificent, old, low-mileage, silver-and-black convertible and have never regretted the impulse purchase.

Ben Stein would understand. In 1971, as a young federal bureaucrat, the comic actor purchased a restored red 1962 Corvette and took to driving 120 miles per hour with his girlfriend along deserted highways. "When I pulled up at stoplights in it, women winked at me," he recalls with nostalgia. "I let my hair grow. I quit my Washington job. . . . It was bliss." The bliss ended when the car's roof leaked and the brakes faded, and he crashed: "It began to dawn on me that the Corvette was not prudent." So Ben bought sensible cars from then on and lost his passion. He became cautious like his father, the famed economist Herb Stein.

After his parents died, Ben reflected on the wisdom they had bequeathed him and decided that they regretted not having taken more chances to enjoy life: "I think my father and mother were saying that it is later than any of us dare to think. If we are going to go for it, do it now. . . . Life is an unbelievable rip-off. . . . Instead of getting the reward of doing what you're passionate about, you awaken to find out that you're fresh out of passion. . . . Life is so incredibly short and those moments in the little red Corvette are so very long."[33]

After years of misfortune, God blessed Job. He died old and full of years, relishing life. Heaven can and will wait. Follow your passion now.

6. To Love and to Cherish:

Savor the Present Moment

The present contains all that there is. It is holy ground.
—Alfred North Whitehead, "Dialogues"[1]

If we love one another, God lives in us and his love is made
complete in us.
—1 John 4:12

The only sure things in life, we're told, are death and taxes, but they are things most of us worry least about. Only about one in four Americans frets about dying, but two-thirds of us worry about ending our days in a nursing home because of physical frailty or long-term illness. Worry is the greatest enemy of a satisfied life, followed by lack of preparation for inevitable setbacks.

As you celebrate the rest of your life you will have less to worry about not because there is less to your life (there will be much more) but because you will have refined your expectations and established your priorities. Instead of waiting for tragedies to strike, you will live confidently counting your blessings. You will be a problem solver rather than a victim.

Instead of wallowing in regret for the past and worrying about the future, you will find serenity in activity, living fully in the present moment, which is the closest approximation of eternity.

In 1860 the Victorian poet and painter Dante Gabriel Rossetti married Elizabeth Eleanor Siddal, a beautiful woman who appears in many paintings of the Pre-Raphaelites. Already suffering from tuberculosis, she died just two years later from an overdose of laudanum. Overcome with grief and remorse for the harsh manner in which he had treated her, the artist thrust into her coffin a book of his unpublished poems as a belated gift of love.

Not many years later, unable to recreate the buried poems from memory, Rossetti had second thoughts about his rash decision, and ordered Elizabeth's coffin exhumed so he could retrieve and publish his poems.

If we can seize on a moral from the poet's morbid decision, it is the one expressed by the author of Ecclesiastes, who affirmed that "there is a time to be born and a time to die" (3:1). True love is expressed better in life than on paper and, during the course of one's lifetime, not after.

As we anticipate our later years, we will cherish even more all that has attracted our affection. If you are fortunate enough to reach retirement in the company of the companion you once vowed to love and cherish, you are blessed, and you are in the majority. Fully 77 percent of men and 51 percent of women between the ages of sixty-five and seventy-four still enjoy the constant companionship of their spouse. Nearly half of men eighty-five and older still share life with their wives.[2]

Incidentally, a 1994 University of Chicago survey revealed that 85 percent of married women and 75 percent of married men have *always* been faithful to their spouses.[3] Far more often than not, love is true. Sigmund Freud was speaking for himself when he exulted, "How bold one gets when one is sure of being loved."[4]

A recent AARP survey shows a sharp rise in divorce among marrieds over the age of fifty. The majority of midlife divorces

(66 percent) are initiated by women. Happily, more than 75 percent of women and 81 percent of men in their fifties found a new serious and exclusive partner, typically within two years of their divorce.[5]

Tennessee Williams affirmed that "the heart is a stubborn organ." The propensity for men and women to remarry after divorce demonstrates the durability of affection, whatever one's age. A landmark Gallup poll reveals that wedded love serves as the foundation of contentment to the end of our lives:

- Most American couples acknowledge themselves to be more in love today that they were in the early years of their marriages.
- Most couples (90 percent) have remained faithful in their marriages.
- Over 80 percent of couples would marry their present spouses if they had to do it all over again.
- Only one in ten marriages encounter serious problems. Those that survive are happier than ever.
- For men and women alike marriage is the single greatest ingredient making for happy lives.[6]

If you are alone, you still possess your life and all creation. You also probably have friends and family, as well as a support group such as your church. Now you will have the time to cherish and savor it. But love of life is single-minded; it does not brook distraction. During our working lives our affections have been scattered among many people and things, some of them unworthy of us. Now we have the leisure to set the value on people and things that they deserve. We can love deeply and cherish wisely.

Because the majority of humankind is impoverished, it concentrates on the avoidance of pain rather than the acquisition of happiness. Even in affluent America, our Puritan heritage inclines many men and women to believe that it is bad to feel good, and that they are moral when they are most uncomfortable. Needless to say, life and love continue to make demands on us, but their rewards far surpass their trials. Seek the good in life in full confidence that you will give pleasure to others as well. Enjoyment, not penance, is the highest expression of gratitude.

The View from Ninety

In an earlier chapter I quoted from a book about aging that Chalmer Roberts wrote at the age of eighty. Today the former *Washington Post* journalist, still active in his nineties, is as ardent as ever in his love of life. "The creaks and groans, the pains and the padding about all are with you when you become a nonagenarian," he acknowledges. "But as they say, consider the alternative and enjoy life. You are a lucky one to be alive."

Roberts's situation is not unique. More than one in four men and women who reach retirement age can expect to reach ninety. A decade ago the reporter wrote that the love of life came down to "keeping your heart pumping, your noodle active, and your mood cheery." He still finds that formula works at ninety—"only slower, more relaxed, tranquil."

Roberts acknowledges that an active old age for couples depends largely on the health of one's spouse. His wife, Lois, broke her hip in her late eighties, so their living space had to be reconfigured to allow her to operate on just one floor with the help of a walker. Roberts still drives and shops, and now he cooks simple meals for the two of them. "I spend more time helping my wife," he notes, "and less on myself. C'est la vie." It helps immeasurably that they are still in love.

"I suppose the key to living in your nineties is to reach that state of serenity that implies a sort of 'above it all' tranquility, that is, unruffled by the exigencies of life, being at peace with the world," he opines. "Maybe it's just the acceptance of the idea that you've already done your damnedest, there's nothing more to do, so take it easy."

Nothing more to do except love and cherish and be grateful. We all want to expand our enjoyment in the autumn of our lives, but it is reassuring to know that when winter is nigh there are still comfortable routines that will make us content at day's end, looking forward to tomorrow.

"After lunch, when I've propped myself up in a comfortable recliner, drowsiness often turns into half an hour's snooze, or more," the nonagenarian confesses. "Then it's five o'clock before you know it. Dinner has to be prepared so we can have our ritual five o'clock drink." Roberts covered presidents for the *Post* from 1953 until 1971, so he ends his day watching the news on television—a professional and personal pleasure.[7] The old newsman, more than most, grasps what the French poet Paul Claudel meant about cherishing the present, rich, fleeting moment—*today*.

Making Love Last

I find few things so disheartening as to see an older couple in a restaurant eating their meal in silence, without a word or gesture to each other. I wonder: can love survive the years?

Yes, but only with effort and devotion. There is a line from one of Shakespeare's sonnets that many couples include in their wedding ceremonies: "Love is not love which alters when it alteration finds."

We are not the same persons we were when we took vows to have and hold one another till death. When the young Abraham Lincoln took Mary Todd to be his wife, he could not predict her fragile hold on sanity, nor could he reckon on the depths of depression to which he would be prone. Yet he inscribed Mary's wedding band, "Love is eternal."

Each of us alters as we age, but while change is inevitable, it does not entail growing apart in the final seasons of our lives. Rather, it means falling in love again with the same person for new reasons. Couples are not unlike comrades in war, defending each other and fighting each other's battles, sharing victories and defeats alike. They are bound by their shared history.

Strictly speaking, marriage is a contract, but few couples embrace wedlock as a purely business proposition. Unlike commercial negotiations, love rests on feelings. Moreover, lovers negotiate with each other as equals, friends, and supporters, not as adversaries. They trust each other, seeking mutual opportunities rather than deals. Whereas success in business consists in getting what you want, love is about getting what you *need*—even when the partners don't completely know at the outset just what that is.

But business negotiations have two advantages over lovers' quarrels: (1) They are guided by law, and (2) they often employ mediators. Whereas, when couples face conflict, they typically lack both guidelines and referees to lead them to agreement.

Making love last rests on respecting differences, accepting apologies, letting go of the past, treading softly on your partner's wounds, and always leaving the door open after disputes. Outsiders instantly recognize good marriages by what intimate couples do: They spend time together, preferring each other's company. They share their interests, their hopes, their vulnerabilities, and their dreams. They complement each other, helping each other to grow as persons. They touch each other, and not just in the bedroom.

Psychologists agree that, among human passions, anger and anxiety are more intense than love and joy. They destroy relationships. So do silence, indifference, and manipulation. Anyone entering a loving relationship expecting to change his beloved is doomed to disappointment. When psychologist Barbara De

Angelis suggests rules for women seeking life partners, most of them turn out to be the same ones that bind couples for a lifetime. Here are some of her precepts:

- Treat others the way you want them to treat you.
- Remember that the opposite sex needs as much love and reassurance as you do.
- Choose partners who play by the rules.
- Don't play games.
- Be yourself.
- If you care, express your feelings.
- Ask questions before you become involved.
- Don't become involved with partners who aren't completely available.
- Look for a person with good character.
- Pay attention to warning signs of possible problems.
- Judge persons by the size of their hearts, not the size of their wallets.
- Be fair. Don't practice double standards.
- Don't fall in love with a partner's potential.
- Be honest about your feelings.
- Show your most attractive feature—your mind.
- Be emotionally generous, not emotionally stingy.
- Put emotional intimacy before sexual intimacy.
- Love, honor, and respect—and expect the same in return.
- Be monogamous, develop a partnership, and spend the rest of your life together.[8]

To these I would add: share similar values, pray for the same blessings, and keep yourself interesting.

Sexuality in Marriage

One thing to prepare for is your sex life after retirement. On average, men and women over sixty-five enjoy sex only about one-third as frequently as much younger couples. Still, one-third of spouses aged sixty-five to seventy-four have intercourse every week and report greater satisfaction than couples who enjoy each other less often.[9] The relative infrequency of love-making among older couples does not mean they have lost interest in sex or in each other, but it's good to keep in practice and not take each other for granted. Physical love depends on collaboration and reciprocity. It is also demanding, because we cannot consume love; we must *make* it. Indeed, divorce among older couples is relatively rare, and fidelity is common. Sex, if less frequent, can be better, not worse. When you and I were young ourselves, we could not imagine our elders locked in passion, but now that we are older ourselves, we can accept that physical attraction outlasts youth.

Without disputing the gratification offered by sex, a case can be made that its need is highly overrated. A man or woman who enjoys intercourse twice a week between the ages of eighteen and seventy-two will have reached peak ecstasy for a total of only nine hours and twenty minutes over an entire lifetime. Over the same period, he or she will have enjoyed 61,320 meals plus snacks and treats too numerous to mention.

Scientists agree that sexual desire is less a function of our bodies than our minds. Unfortunately, couples who are otherwise comfortable with each other often allow their sex life to become so routine and predictable that its prospect no longer excites them. Although sex is mostly in our minds, we also need to pay attention to remaining fit as we age.

A Dangerous Love and an Unmarried Compromise

In anticipation of spending more time together, romantic love centers on one's spouse, and physical affection can be more gratifying than ever.

Still, because half of all marriages fail at some point, many men and women approach retirement unconnected, yet sexually active. They are at risk. Men and women aged fifty and older now account for more than one in seven of all new AIDS cases diagnosed annually. The disease is overwhelmingly transmitted by heterosexual relations—a 94 percent rise in older men and 106 percent increase in older women just between 1991 and 1996.[10]

Older men, until recently prone to impotence, now extend their sex lives thanks to Viagra and its clones. Because divorced women past menopause need not worry about pregnancy, they tend not to insist on their intimate partners using a condom. What is most alarming is that doctors seldom think of testing seniors for HIV. Sexually active seniors themselves compound the problem by mistaking AIDs-related symptoms as just part of the aging process, whereas they may be dying prematurely of a disease popularly associated with promiscuous youngsters, homosexuals, or IV-drug users.

Increasingly, divorced and widowed seniors are electing to live together without benefit of marriage. The 2000 census reveals that cohabitation by seniors doubled in the last decade of the twentieth century, outstripping the increase among younger age groups. Mature couples are motivated more by pragmatism than romance. Two can live more cheaply than one, and by forgoing wedlock, partners avoid the financial obligations of each other's long-term medical care and losing their own retirement benefits as well.

Typically, cohabiting seniors provide for each other in their wills, but not for their partner's adult children. Ruth Nippe, seventy-nine, has lived with Jim McDaniel, eighty-one, without marriage for four years. She explains: "At our age we have to think about when one of us isn't going to be here. Even though I'm very good friends with his kids, I wouldn't be comfortable if they ended up owning half of my house."[11]

Demographers expect that baby boomers who rebelled in their twenties will carry on their love for individual freedom, further shrinking the number of partners who opt for marriage in their later years.

The Satisfactions of Friendship

Romance is not the only kind of affection. Aristotle exalted friendship as a virtue and "one of the most indispensable requirements of life." Cicero went even further: "Without friendship," he said, "life is not worth living." Blood may be thicker than water, but friendship is not nearly as burdened by emotion and expectation as family ties. Romantic love is by its nature exclusive and possessive, whereas friendship is open and free. Marriage is bound by contract, whereas friendship is voluntary and free, beyond legal and formal control.

Becky and I each have a best friend. She hasn't seen hers in years, but they e-mail each other daily, talk on the phone, and write often, sharing books, gifts, advice, recipes, and laughter. Although my friend lives closer, we too seldom see each other, but still keep in constant touch. A friend is a reliable asset.

When I returned to Illinois to attend my fortieth college class reunion, I hadn't seen most of my classmates for that many years, yet we picked up on our conversations as if commencement had been only yesterday. Becky went through elementary and high school with the same group of girls. Today many of them are grandmothers. The classmates join together every year and correspond by e-mail nearly every week. One summer they gathered in our small Virginia home. Many brought sleeping bags and pillows and slept wherever they could find space on the floor. They provided one another a weekend of laughter and fun.

Surely one of the most satisfying aspects of later life is the opportunity to enjoy old friends and cultivate new ones. Acquaintances abound, but friends are different. During our working lives, we tend to socialize with co-workers, but later on we can find friends anywhere and have the time and leisure to enjoy them. Friends offer commitment, candor, trust, honesty, and commonality, delightfully free from emotional demands.

Not many years ago Becky and I became Friends—the kind with a capital "F"—joining a Quaker meeting a half-hour drive from our home. Most Friends are Christians like ourselves, but our small meeting includes a sprinkling of Jews, Buddhists, Muslims, and people who share our values but are still searching for a religious faith. We are all joined in the belief that there is something of God in every human being, and that we are responsible for one another and for the world's people. That is a sound basis for friendship.

In active retirement you will no longer have your workplace as a source of companionship. If you have children, they will be adults leading their own lives and cultivating their own friends. So you will have to exert the effort to nurture a new circle of men and women whose company you enjoy and who can be a source of support and comfort.

Churches still afford people the opportunity to socialize, to share values and experiences, and to assist one another. Lending assistance and giving pleasure are much the same thing. But it is as easy to compartmentalize worship and fellowship as anything else in life. Socializing on the Sabbath is not enough. We need compatible friends to nourish us, to protect us from getting stuck in our ways, and to prevent us from growing old prematurely.

Church, synagogue, and mosque are traditional sources for friendship, but so too are hobbies and sports. Trekkies, I'm told, make fast friends at Star Trek conventions. But friendship doesn't just happen; it must be cultivated. So lower your drawbridge and fill in your moat. Get out and cultivate friends.

Business or Pleasure?

International travelers are greeted by customs officers with the question, "Are you here for business or pleasure?" In the rest of our lives we must not hesitate to answer "pleasure." Our enjoyment of life is the best sign of gratitude for its gift.

Rutgers University anthropologist Lionel Tiger asks rhetorically, "What is wrong with hedonism, so long as people turn up for work on time, obey traffic signals, recycle beer cans, and do not abuse the welfare and dignity of others?"[12] In our later years we will hopefully no longer need to show up at work at all, so we will encounter even fewer impediments to life's enjoyment. If happiness is a habit you have not yet acquired, it is worth practicing.

David G. Myers is a psychologist who has devoted his life to dissecting the traits happy people share. Here is his list:

- fit and healthy bodies
- realistic goals and expectations
- positive self-esteem
- feelings of control
- optimism
- outgoingness
- supportive friendships that enable companionship and confiding
- a socially intimate, sexually warm, equitable marriage
- challenging work and active leisure, punctuated by adequate rest and retreat
- a faith that entails communal support, purpose, acceptance, outward focus, and hope[13]

Unfortunately, none of these happy traits comes in a gift package, nor can they be purchased. But all can be achieved, even late in life.

Psychologists agree that if you start acting "as if" you are happy, you will find that contentment can become a habit like any other. Granted, pleasure-seeking can be abused at any stage in life, but only if we are frivolous in our enjoyments or too demanding of our senses. Excessive indulgence of taste can lead to gluttony, just as a demanding sex life can lead to promiscuity and worse. The connoisseur of fine wine, art, music, reading, beauty, and nature does not overindulge his or her passion.

Basic Pleasures

There is a universal temptation to feel deprived and to suspect that other people have more to love and cherish than we do. My father, the mildest of men, persuaded himself that, were it not for the responsibilities of work and family, and the constraints of Christianity, he would have been the greatest playboy in the Western world. Instead, he was dutiful and indulged simple loves. In growing season Dad would pick a flower from our garden and wear it in his buttonhole all day at the office. That small gesture acknowledged the gifts of his Creator and made his day's work more a piece with the rest of his life.

Despite our fantasies about freedom to indulge ourselves in retirement, most Americans do not move to warm weather paradises but remain contentedly for as long as possible in the homes in which they pursued their working lives. They realize that friends, neighbors, churches, and familiar places offer more reliable pleasures than life on a beach or golf course. Revealingly, the lives of the rich and famous, although pleasant, are often pro-saic. William Shatner, who, as Captain James Kirk of the Starship Enterprise ventured where no man had gone before, confides that in real life he is a stay-at-home person: "I don't live an extravagant lifestyle. I don't attend lavish soirees in the south of France, or black-tie events in Manhattan. I stay home. I don't have champagne wishes or caviar dreams. . . . I'm thrilled if my *fries* are supersized. Give me a takeout pizza, a couch full of dogs, and a rented Jackie Chan video, and I'm happy as a clam."[14] Shatner lives in Kentucky rather than Beverly Hills because he raises horses, his one real luxury.

Peter Mayle, whose book, *A Year in Provence*, tempted a recent generation of Americans to pull up stakes and move to the south of France in retirement, is a sybarite's icon. Yet he, too, protests: "I have one house, one small car, one bicycle, and four seldom-worn suits. Food and wine, since I'm lucky to live in an agricultural area of southern France, are good and inexpensive. My vices are relatively cheap, and I spend more money on books than anything else. I have no wish for a yacht, a racehorse, a butler, or even a crocodile attaché case with solid brass fittings and a combination lock, let alone the possessions that really gobble money—a vineyard in Bordeaux, for instance, or a collection of Impressionist art. I can admire and appreciate all these wonderful things, but I don't want to own them. They are, as far as I am concerned, more trouble than they're worth. They end up owning you."[15]

A few years ago I set about writing a book about the pursuit of happiness. When I finished *Spiritual Simplicity*, it turned out to be a recipe for simple living with a large dose of spirituality. This book is its logical sequel. Along the way I have discovered, as Mayle did before me, that nonessential possessions weigh one down and distract the mind and senses, which need to be free to seek contentment. From time to time we need to conduct a substantial yard sale to rid ourselves of possessions we no longer love and cherish because they no longer satisfy.

What's Wrong with the World?

Years ago, when the *Times* of London asked prominent pundits of the day to submit essays on the topic, "What's wrong with the world?" The Christian convert G. K. Chesterton responded to the question with a single word: "Me!"[16]

He was answering, of course, not only for himself but for human nature. Chesterton was persuaded that people spoil the world for themselves and for one another by being self-centered and shortsighted. He argued that the most rewarding pleasures at any age come from pleasing others.

Formal invitations to gatherings used to request "the pleasure of your company." Hosts could expect their guests to provide that pleasure. Long before movies, television, and video games converted us into solitary couch potatoes, people entertained one another by their conversation, companionship, and simple presence. Reading a nineteenth-century guest book discovered in a Connecticut home we borrowed one summer, I was struck by the sentiments visitors recorded there, expressing gratitude to their hosts and fellow guests for pleasant sojourns and good company. Clearly, people once took pleasure in one another and were openly grateful for companionship.

Americans of all ages still socialize, of course, but much of human interaction today revolves around business, sports, children, or other agendas. Every Saturday in fair weather our local school's playing field plays host to hundreds of tiny soccer players and their cheering parents. Lamentably, the games are not occasions for couples to enjoy the company of other adults. Their kids' competition is the only point for harried soccer moms and dads to gather in the same place at the same time.

Early in my career, when I first became a supervisor, I was advised not to socialize much with my staff, lest I be accused of granting favors to some and not to others. In retrospect, I must admit it was sound counsel, because I had to make painful employment decisions about some colleagues whom I really liked. But that self-imposed barrier severely restricted my circle of friends. Soon I found myself wearing one face to work and another in my personal life.

I am haunted by a study made by Robert Bellah (published as *Habits of the Heart*), in which the sociologist profiles an American population that, despite material comforts, lacks a language in which to express its longings, moral purposes, and the point of their lives. People who cannot please themselves cannot please others.[17] Bellah's profile was more recently sustained by Robert D. Putnam in *Bowling Alone*. For the rest of our lives, let us vow to be the kind of persons who please. It will provide us with much, and many, to love and cherish.

Having and Holding More

A common misconception about aging is that we will have less than before and gradually lose our hold on what remains. Granted, we will no longer have promotions and an expanding income, the sense of accomplishment that comes with a paying job, or children to nurture. But we will enjoy the better bargain: the gift of *time*, and the freedom to translate time into aspiration and involvement.

But be warned: the generation of Americans now approaching retirement has largely disengaged from community and social life. The baby boom generation cherishes a "do-it-yourself" independence. Because the satisfaction it seeks is largely solitary, retirement could mean a lonely retreat from active life.

Harvard University sociologist Robert D. Putnam characterizes this detachment from involvement as "bowling alone"—also the title of his best-selling study of our disengagement from society. His findings include the following:

- Baby boomers belong to only half as many civic organizations as did their grandparents.
- They express less than half the trust in other people as did their grandparents.
- They vote at only half the rate as their elders.
- They express only half as much interest in politics.
- They are only half as likely to attend church regularly or to volunteer on community projects.
- They are only one-third as likely to read a daily newspaper as their elders.[18]

The Pleasure of Their Company

There are 500 million living creatures in American homes in addition to the humans who live there. They are pets (mostly dogs and cats), and they are a pleasure. Animals ask for little, seldom complain, and display a loyalty worthy of a saint. Whereas humans are often beastly, beasts are simply natural.

At our house we enjoy the constant companionship of two cats and a Scottish terrier. When we exchange homes with other couples, Becky and I are delighted to care for their pets. (In England we have even enjoyed the companionship of foxes.) In later life your contentment may come to you on four paws or even on the wing. Animals are a joy, a comfort, and only a modest responsibility. As a girl, Becky had a pet lamb, whereas my mother's final years were brightened by a canary's song. Mom named the bird "Happy," for it made her so. Pets can make us happy, too.

At the Creation, God affirmed that it is not good for humans to be alone. Yet many of us can look forward to spending the last years of our lives without the comforting presence of spouse and children. The remedy for companionship can be found at your nearest animal shelter. A veterinarian friend of mine provides pets to convicts behind bars. It is a ministry that affords even hardened criminals the opportunity to love and cherish.

I often ponder how our own dog and cats manage to act out their natures so beautifully, when people find it such a trial to act human. Pets are the easiest antidote to human loneliness. By their dependence on us, they make us responsible for them and more responsible to ourselves. Perhaps the final companion in your later years will possess a tail!

Being Rich

Abraham Lincoln was persuaded that "most people are as happy as they make up their minds to be." George Bernard Shaw claimed, "The way to have a happy life is to be so busy doing what you like all the time that there is no time left to think about whether you are happy."

In retirement you will have more time to be reflective, but it is no time to brood. It helps to count our blessings and open our hearts and senses. Unless you are deaf you must listen to the birds' songs. Unless you are blind you cannot escape beauty. At day's end it is pleasant to sleep, and each morning it is good to wake. Our minds are sponges ready to absorb the next item of interest and the occasional bit of wisdom. Our senses are made for enjoyment. The world is our playground. For such a life the only appropriate response is gratitude.

Anthropologist Lionel Tiger celebrates the pervasiveness and inevitability of joy at any age:

> Certain large themes of human existence are difficult to avoid.
> They ring in the ear. Pleasure resonates as an imperative.
> There is no choice but to expect it, experience it, enjoy it.

We could not have survived the dark nights and bright days of our immense story without it. It was a guide, a lure, a road sign to an oasis. Its enjoyment summarized good and successful choices, and its experience was a confirmation. It was and is central to our deepest accountancy, finally as clear-cut as the mysterious certainty of soaring music. Pleasure as guide, pleasure as proof, pleasure as tonic, pleasure as festivity, pleasure as fun and triumph. There's no choice. We have to have pleasure.[19]

Not everyone would agree. Living well may be our last and best revenge, but pleasure seeking can make us frivolous and distract us from deeper joy. Robert Barclay, the seventeenth-century Quaker theologian, condemned not only violence, but "games, sports, plays, comedies, or other recreations which are inconsistent with Christian silence or gravity." He specifically condemned "drunkenness, whoring, and riotousness" and would probably encounter no argument on those latter counts.[20] But today there is an old upright piano in our old Quaker meetinghouse, and Friends occasionally burst into song during otherwise silent worship. Children play hide-and-seek in the little graveyard behind the house, and there is much laughter among the adults.

As a child, Becky was taught the poem:

Quaker meeting has begun.
No more laughing, no more fun.
If you dare to crack a smile,
You will have to walk a mile.

As maturing adults, we have discovered otherwise. The gentle Friends delight in the human comedy, laughing first of all at themselves. They are grateful for simple gifts, not least for the gift of being able to love and cherish one another, as well as life itself for as long as it lasts.

Because he possessed faith, hope, and love, Saint Paul, chained in prison and prepared for death, could nevertheless promise, "My God will meet all your needs according to his glorious riches in Christ Jesus" (Philippians 4:19). He was speaking to all of us.

7. To Have and to Hold:

Cherish Your Friends and Companions

Love is eternal.
—Inscribed in Mary Todd Lincoln's wedding band[1]

"Peace I leave with you; my peace I give you. . . . Do not let your hearts be troubled and do not be afraid."
—John 14:27

Perhaps the greatest compliment Jesus of Nazareth ever paid his followers was to call them his friends. "I no longer call you servants," he told his apostles, "because a servant does not know his master's business. Instead, I have called you friends" (John 15:15).

My wife and I worship with Quakers, who describe themselves as the Religious Society of Friends. I suspect we are blessed with more "friends" than many other Americans, if for no other reason than it's how we address one another.

Samuel Taylor Coleridge called friendship "a sheltering tree." C. S. Lewis lamented that the modern world ignores the unselfish bond between friends. Christianity has always hallowed love as the greatest of virtues, and friendship is love's practical expression, knowing no distinction as to gender, class, or even age. Friendship is based on a *commonality of interest, affection, mutual concern and responsibility. Friends can rely on one another.*

You may have only one spouse, whereas you can make many friends as you celebrate the rest of your life.

The Bible affirms that there is a time to love and a time to die. Fair enough. Autumn is life's season for having and holding.

I set about writing this book with just two readers in mind—my wife and myself—trusting that whatever we discovered about living wisely and lovingly in our later years would apply to you and to our contemporaries.

Becky and I are determined to have and to hold one another and all God's gifts that come our way—not to let life and love fritter away as the days grow short. But sentiment is not enough; planning is needed. I am married to a woman more than a decade my junior, and women have a life expectancy longer than men. Becky could easily look forward to another twenty or more years of life once I'm gone. I share responsibility with her for the quality of life she will enjoy during those years before we are rejoined in heaven.

One weekend in my workaholic middle age, Becky gave me an ultimatum. "David, you're killing yourself," she said. "You insist on handling the family finances. If you dropped dead tomorrow, I wouldn't know what to do." On the spot she made me promise to spell out on paper exactly the steps she will have to take the instant I am out of the picture and she is alone.

It was a humbling but necessary wake-up call, and ever since I have lived a saner, healthier life. But I also did as she demanded and wrote a detailed script so she can handle affairs without me. Our wills are up-to-date. We have given power of attorney to each other in case one of us becomes incapacitated, and we both have living wills to ensure that our lives are not unduly extended in terminal illness. Our doctor knows of our wishes. We belong to the local memorial society and know where we can be laid to rest simply and with dignity at modest expense.

During Becky's working life, she accounted for much of the retirement savings on which we depend. If the U.S. economy does not go into total collapse, she will have enough income to live comfortably, if modestly, without relying on our children. Our wills are written to cover even the possibility of our dying together in an accident.

Of course, it is impossible to completely plan one's own life, let alone those of our survivors. Life is full of surprises, not all of them welcome. But over the years I have seen too many people die alone, and in mean circumstances, because they abandoned their later years to fate. Short of consulting a fortune teller, however, one can set up contingencies.

When predicaments present themselves and solutions are elusive, Becky asks, "What is the worst thing that could happen?" trusting that if we can conceive of the worst, we can manage anything less dire. So can you, by confronting some likely and less likely scenarios.

Housing and Long-term Care

To ensure the rest of our lives will be worthy of celebration, we will have to adjust to new physical realities as they occur. Spiritual maturity requires us to accept new necessities in a good spirit.

For example, assuming you live as a couple, if one of you becomes less mobile, will you be able to afford to reconfigure your present living space, or will you have to move to a one-floor living arrangement? When the husband of a former colleague of mine was no longer able to walk unassisted, the couple installed an elevator in their Georgetown home along with other safety features. Those modifications cost as much as the value of Becky's and my modest house!

Louis Tenenbaum, a Maryland contractor who specializes in remodeling homes for seniors and the disabled, estimates that modifications to an existing home can cost up to $182,000.

Doing nothing is *not* an option. Falls alone rank as the sixth-leading cause of death among people over sixty-five. Short of death, tumbles often result in fractures that are a leading cause of disability and force people unwillingly out of their homes into nursing facilities. When I turned sixty-five I reluctantly took out a long-term care policy that extends Medicare coverage in a nursing home should I become disabled. But the policy's premium is a burden on our budget, and I'm not sanguine about the prospect of living in a nursing home anyway.

A wise move to guard against slips and falls in your home as you grow older is to install solid grips in your bathrooms and banisters in stairwells where they are missing. You can make these safety improvements now at little expense. Make certain that carpets are secure on the floor, and take to wearing rubber-soled shoes and slippers. Use a rubber bath mat to ensure against falls while bathing or showering. If you live in a multilevel home with outdoor stairs, install a handrail. These small safety improvements now can prevent an accident later that might lead to disability.

John Mortimer, the playwright, is confined to a wheelchair because of a series of accidents he could have avoided. First, he skipped down a flight of stairs to answer his door, breaking his leg. Then his Achilles tendon gave way during a too-hard game of tennis. "As a result of an operation to rejuvenate it," he sighs, "my other leg swelled up like a balloon, contracting a thrombosis." Later he tumbled from a terrace while gardening, causing an ulcerated leg, and ripped his knee muscles slipping down lavatory steps. "All over the world," he surmises, "men and women who have experienced a reasonable quantity of life are toppling over, collapsing in kitchens or hurtling down stairs."

Reflecting on his own experience, Mortimer predicts that "the time will come in your life, it will almost certainly come, when the voice of God will thunder at you from a cloud, 'From this day forth thou shalt not be able to put on thine own socks.'"[2]

Mutual Support

So who will help you into your socks? And why should they bother? A pollster once put it to Mortimer's wife, Penny: "He really is getting old, isn't he; why do you stay with John? Is it love or duty?" She replied, "Probably both."

Mortimer's own mother put up with her ill-tempered blind spouse in his old age, dressing him, cutting up his food, reading to him, and leading him about, substituting for his eyes by keeping up a running commentary about their surroundings.

Of his long-suffering wife and mother, Mortimer asks, "Why do they do it? Does love really survive bad temper and failing joints? Is it a point of honor to stand by our friends and relations? Is staying on to put on other people's socks the mark of a truly heroic character? I would say, undoubtedly, yes."[3]

Such devotion is not limited to wives. A former colleague of mine observed his wife become a total invalid to Alzheimer's disease. He nursed her for years until her death. When the beautiful actress Rita Hayworth was afflicted with the same disease, her daughter, Princess Yasmin Khan, devoted herself totally to caring for her mother until she died.

When I was growing up, it was not uncommon for American households to consist of three generations. Today, when many couples must both work outside the home to make ends meet, it is difficult enough to arrange day care for the children without also managing to care for an aging parent within their four walls.

For years, my mother's blind father shared our tiny apartment, while my father's mother was cared for by her brother. It is sad to note that many men and women currently living in nursing homes are not disabled. Their children's hectic lifestyles can't accommodate caring for aging parents in their own homes.

In recent years it has become common for young singles to live in group homes, because they can't yet afford apartments of their own. Group homes for seniors make sense for the same reason, with the additional advantage of mutual support. God affirmed that it is not good for man to be alone—a truth that applies to aging women as well. Although my wife is independent-minded, it is unlikely that she would choose to maintain our home alone or live a solitary life anywhere, but would opt to share an apartment or home with a friend (and many pets). Her female high school classmates have entertained the notion of sharing a house if they are widowed.

When Becky and I were members of St. Alban's parish in Northwest Washington, D.C., we became aware that the high-rise buildings in the neighborhood were home to hundreds of widows, most of them financially comfortable but living solitary lives in their small apartments. Few were acquainted with fellow seniors in their own buildings. With the help of the clergy and older couples in our parish, we introduced the widows to their nearest neighbors and ensured that they would at least check on one another from time to time by phone.

How Others Manage

In Italy it is not uncommon for a poor widow or widower to be taken in by an unrelated family, in return for helping with the children and mentioning the host family in his or her will. In warm climates, older people can entertain themselves contentedly out of doors. John Mortimer, who spends summers in Italy, explains: "Old men are taken to the café. A chair is set for them, usually at the point where the tables meet the traffic, so they are half in and half out of the way. They sit with their hands folded over their sticks, only occasionally exchanging greetings or complaints, doing absolutely nothing until it is time for them to be taken home, fed a little, and put to bed."[4]

I suppose Mortimer means to paint a pathetic scene, but it strikes me as more attractive than sitting at home alone, staring into space, or seeking companionship at McDonald's or the mall. In comparison, the prospect of soaking up the sun and surveying the passing scene in a Tuscan village square sounds good to me. Of course, it's an unlikely prospect. We live here, not there.

Assuming Medicare coverage improves, it will become more common for aging Americans to receive care in their own homes. There are even home computers today that can periodically monitor your health and transmit the information to your physician's office without the need to pay him or her a visit.

The hospice movement is probably the most promising innovation in care for the aging during their last six to twelve months of life. The aim is to provide holistic care—medical, physical, emotional, and spiritual—in one's home or in homelike surroundings, not only to the older person or couple, but to all members of the family, at minimum expense. Ernest Morgan explains: "In the Middle Ages hospice was the name given to a place of refuge—an inn—where travelers could refresh themselves on their journeys. The name was given a new meaning when St. Christopher's Hospice was formed in London in 1967 by Cicely Saunders. Hospice then became a place where the dying could live their remaining days as fully and comfortably as possible, surrounded by loved ones, free from pain, and dying with dignity."[5]

The hospice team typically consists of a physician and nurse plus a social worker and pastor, assisted by helpful volunteers. To contact the hospice organization nearest to you, contact your local health department or call Hospice Helpline (800-658-8898).

Mutual Trust and Generosity

When the United States employs military force or enforces trade sanctions against other nations, it explains that it is protecting its "vital interests." When it offers foreign aid to poor nations, it acknowledges its motive to be "enlightened self-interest."

In both cases, the nation acts for self-centered reasons. Unfortunately, many Americans believe that selfishness motivates individuals as well as nations. That suspicion makes us wary and untrusting of one another, especially as we grow older and more dependent on others. In her final years, my mother took to tipping the employees of her nursing home for simply doing their jobs. In essence, her tips were bribes, because she believed people could only be motivated to serve others by money.

We are quick to sell human nature short. People don't have to be saints to be trustworthy and to do good. Goodness, after all, is not so much a matter of character as it is of effective behavior. Ordinary flawed people do a world of good.

When the *Washington Post* told the story of Amber Coffman, a teenage beauty queen who distributes thirty-six thousand sandwiches a year to the destitute in Baltimore, it implied that she must have mixed motives, because her generosity attracted attention and could conceivably help her career. Stunned by the criticism, Amber protested that she is only trying to help the less fortunate. Whatever one suspects about her motives, what matters is that stomachs once empty are now full.

We will never trust others if we assume that they are at heart self-serving. Doubtless, self-preservation is a basic human instinct, but we are seldom so desperate that it becomes our overriding motive. Most people are cautious but generous. Once we acknowledge that fact, we become more trusting and generous ourselves. We attract friends and make the world a better place.

Americans contribute over $240 billion each year to good causes. In addition, ninety-three million Americans volunteer their time regularly to helping others, working over twenty billion hours a year, worth another $200 billion. Surprisingly, teenagers are even more generous with their time than their parents. Nearly 60 percent of American teens volunteer an average 3.5 hours of their time each week to helping those in need.[6]

As we age, living on a fixed income, we cannot extend our generosity to as many charities as we would like. But while we must be more selective, we need not be stingy, especially with our time, of which we now have an abundance. If you don't already do so, consider volunteering some of your time to a good cause, preferably one that brings you face to face with people in need.

Don't get hung up deciding whether a beggar is deserving or undeserving of your generosity. Anyone reduced to begging is less fortunate than we are. During the Great Depression, the humorist Fred Allen never left home without a pocketful of quarters, giving them to anyone who asked. During the years Becky worked on Capitol Hill, the same homeless man approached her every day for a handout. "Most days none of my coworkers offered me a word of thanks," she recalls, "and none ever said 'God bless you.' But the beggar did." That was motivation enough to prompt her generosity.

Faith

The confidence we will need to navigate the rest of our lives flows from faith in ourselves, which begins with self-knowledge. "Explore thyself!" Thoreau urges us all. Shakespeare's Hamlet marveled at the human animal: "What a piece of work is man! How noble in reason! How infinite in faculty! in form and loving how express and admirable! in action how like an angel! in apprehension how like a god! the beauty of the world! the paragon of animals!"

Yet in the next breath the prince's faith in humanity and himself faltered: "And yet, to me, what is this quintessence of dust?"[7]

Hamlet's faith in humanity and himself lacked hope and love. You will want to nurture a faith that secures your future and engages your affections as well as your mind. For that you will need a faith in something—or someone—outside yourself.

If you conceive of yourself as a mere accidental speck of life in a vast, impersonal universe, you are not likely to find a faith that holds out much hope. Believers and doubters are equally exposed to life's trials, but the believer knows where he stands in the universe and where he is going.

No one can live free of faith. If you or I attempted to live confidently on the basis of what we know for an absolute fact, we could never get out of bed in the morning to face the uncertain day. People cannot help but live by faiths that fall short of certitude, but we can shed false faiths that are built of little more than habit and sentiment, and we can build a faith full of hope.

Take the time to list your beliefs on a single sheet of paper, starting with what you believe about yourself. What kind of person do you think you are? Then ask yourself what you do daily to justify your faith in yourself. For example, if you consider yourself a truthful person, what hard truths have you revealed or confronted lately? If you think of yourself as generous, what acts of kindness have you displayed of late? Next answer this: What do I believe in *beyond* myself? In what or whom do I place my faith?

Then summon the courage to submit your findings to a couple of trusted friends. Do they see you the way you see yourself? If not, don't despair. Your faith may be fine. It may be only your self-image that is faulty. Even saints falter in action, but they maintain their faith despite their shortcomings. To be worthy of your adherence, your faith needs to be *bigger* and *better* than you alone.

Francis of Assisi was once challenged by a peasant who had heard of the friar's generosity. He urged the saint: "Try to be as good as people think you are." From all reports Francis succeeded. Despite a life of almost inconceivable deprivation and generosity, he became the happiest man who has ever lived.[8]

The Meaning of Your Life

If you look up my entry in *Who's Who in America*, you will find statistics, such as my birthplace and date, the names of my wife and children, the schools I attended, the jobs I've held, awards I've won, and titles of books I've written to date. But nowhere will you find a mention of my faith or values—whether I'm a coward or a cad, generous or stingy, attentive or preoccupied, gregarious or friendless, and whether I possess a sense of humor. It is chilling to acknowledge that when I die, some anonymous obituary writer will borrow from that meager entry to summarize the significance of my life.

In your own career you probably composed a resume that was just as inadequate to describe who you are. When you reach retirement, it's time to discard your work resume and set down on paper an account of the people and the pleasures that make your life worth living. In fact, it's time to choose an epitaph for yourself before someone else chooses it for you. It is a mistake to leave it to others to take the measure of your life after you are gone.

Many celebrated men and women are careful to write their memoirs to cast their lives in the most favorable light and head off revisionists who think less of them than they do of themselves. A noteworthy exception to assertive celebrity was Jesus of Nazareth, who wrote nothing about himself and left it to his friends to tell us who he was. But Jesus knew himself and what his life was about. To live fully, you need to reflect on who you are and what you stand for. It's time to write your epitaph.

"But my life is not over," you may object. "How can I take the measure of it?" To which I answer: by that time it will be too late. Writing your epitaph is an exercise in separating what is important to you from what is merely ephemeral, then projecting your true values to the end of your life. Although the Creator gave us life, we create its shape and give it direction. Our power of creativity is our likeness to God.

When at the end of your earthly sojourn a eulogist or obituary writer composes an appreciation of your life, what do you want it to say? Look back over your life and acknowledge your accomplishments, failures, aspirations, and satisfactions, and recall the people who have been and are important to you. Put it on paper, and it will serve as the script for the rest of your life. Without that script, you will be unable to appreciate the gifts you have already been given and those that will bring you the greatest joy throughout the final seasons of your life.

On our travels, Becky and I have toured old cemeteries in Britain and America, touched by the sentiments carved on crumbling stone by survivors who not only grieved but celebrated the lives of the deceased. In these peaceful places lie not just human remains but "devoted husbands," "faithful wives," and "cherished children." The sentiments make the difference, and they are full of hope. Consider these lines carved in the headstone of a young man who died of yellow fever in New Orleans a century and a half ago:

But why indulge these notes of grief,
Why should we thus complain?
What now to us is less severe
Is his eternal gain.

Loving Your Life

When Henry David Thoreau abandoned his solitary life at Walden Pond, he gave this explanation: "I left the woods for as good a reason as I went there. . . . I had several more lives to live, and could not spare any more time for that one. It is remarkable how easily and insensibly we fall into a particular route, and make a beaten track for ourselves."[9]

The hermit of Walden returned to society but carried Walden's wisdom with him the rest of his life: "I learned this, at least, in my experiment: that if one advances confidently in the direction of his dreams, and endeavors to live the life which he has imagined, he will meet with a success unexpected in common hours. He will put some things behind, will pass an invisible boundary; new, universal, and more liberal laws will begin to establish themselves around and within him."[10]

But that revelation requires human investment: "In proportion as he simplifies his life, the laws of the universe will appear less complex, and solitude will not be solitude, nor poverty poverty, nor weakness weakness. If you have built castles in the air, your work need not be lost; that is where they should be. Now put the foundations under them."[11]

"Love your life," Thoreau urges us. "Meet it and live it; do not shun it and call it hard names. . . . The fault-finder will find faults even in paradise."

Thoreau continues, "Things do not change; we change. Sell your clothes and keep your thoughts. God will see that you do not want society. If I were confined to a corner of a garret all my days, like a spider, the world would be just as large to me while I had my thoughts about me."[12]

Thoreau relates a story about an artist who devoted his life to striving after perfection, only to find eternity: "His singleness of purpose and resolution, and his elevated piety, endowed him, without his knowledge, with perennial youth.

As he made no compromise with Time, Time kept out of his way."[13]

As we journey through life we, too, need make no compromises with the passing years, but discover perennial youth through devotion to life, keeping in mind Thoreau's counsel that "only that day dawns to which we are awake. There is more day to dawn. The sun is but a morning star."[14]

8. Till Death Do Us Part:

Make Peace with Your Mortality

One short sleep past, we wake eternally,
And death shall be no more; death, thou shalt die."
—John Donne, Holy Sonnets, X

Neither death nor life . . . will be able to separate us from the love
of God that is in Christ our Lord.
—Romans 8:38

If you are a celebrity, either famous or infamous, you may rest assured that your death notice has already been written and is waiting patiently in the memory of a computer in some newspaper office for the day of your demise. Unlike other events, a person's death is not exactly news, because it is predictable. All that needs to be filled-in before it goes to print is its cause and your age at the end.

Long before Ronald Reagan's death an Oxford University dean confided in me that he was the author of the former president's obituary, which indeed appeared in Britain's Independent newspaper the morning after Reagan passed into eternity. Every now and then through the decades my friend updated his biographical account, including the president's affliction with Alzheimer's.

In Britain the writing of obituaries is considered an art. It is not uncommon for the nation's broadsheets to carry the posthumous biographies of men and women hardly anyone knew existed when they were alive. But then the British have a love of eccentrics and a wicked sense of humor about life and death.

A few years ago I led a seminar at Pendle Hill in Pennsylvania helping to reconcile a group of middle-aged men and women with their own mortality. One assignment was for each person to write his or her own obituary. The results were encouraging. Instead of resembling a bloodless employment resume, each little autobiography revealed the loves and joys, the people and events, and the love of God that made that person's life worth living.

As you contemplate celebrating the rest of your life, cherish your own blessings.

On the morning of September 11, 2001, architect Katherine Ilachinski, still working at age seventy-one, was in her ninety-first floor office at Two World Trade Center when a jetliner hit the opposite tower just above the level of her office window. Katherine was no stranger to violence. As a girl, she had survived the Nazi bombing of Belgrade, and in 1993 she had been in her World Trade Center office when terrorists exploded a bomb in the skyscraper's basement. Back then she closed her office. Of 2001, she recalls:

> This time, I just wanted to get out of the building [but the airless elevators were mobbed]. That was when I decided to walk, and something just propelled me to the north stairs. I don't know by what force I was propelled. But now . . . I can look at the pictures and see: that was the side least affected by the second jet. Through almost

everything, I felt amazingly calm, except for that one moment in the stairwell, when the building started shaking, and I thought, I'm a goner. I wished I was back on the ninety-first floor, and I could jump. Because I could jump from the window—reluctantly, but I could do it—because then it's over. But to be trapped under rubble, that is worse. I remember, from the war, from Belgrade, what it is to be trapped.

Katherine emerged from the building alive and uninjured, but is haunted by a "guilt feeling you wouldn't believe." She appreciates that she has already lived a long and full life, but "all these young people went . . ."[1]

The vast majority of people acknowledge the inevitability of their eventual demise, are resigned to it, and do not fear it. Some even welcome it. After all, as Lord Byron acknowledged:

Death, so called, is a thing that makes men weep,

And yet a third of life is passed in sleep.[2]

No, what people fear is *dying* itself, because it is an enigma associated with suffering and decline. Moreover, we are helpless to control the timing and the way of our passing—which explains why Katherine Ilachinski expressed a preference for jumping to her death over being trapped in the rubble of the twin towers. After the tragedies, psychologists had a ready explanation for why so many workers had leapt from their windows: because it made them masters of their demise rather than victims—choosing the way if not the time. Some even held hands as they plunged to their death.

Rededicating Ourselves to Life

At the border of the autumn of life, we will not only pause to grieve for friends and family whose lives were cut short prematurely, but also rededicate ourselves to the business of living. Simone de Beauvoir affirms that "it is old age, rather than death, that is to be contrasted with life. Old age is life's parody, whereas death transforms life into a destiny."[3]

In our later years, it is critical that we not *retire* from living but become even more alive. Still, as de Beauvoir acknowledges, "Undergoing age is not an activity. Growing, ripening, aging, dying—the passing of time is predestined, inevitable." She affirms that:

> there is only one solution if old age is not to be an absurd parody of our former life, and that is to go on pursuing ends that give our existence a meaning. . . . In old age we should wish still to have passions strong enough to prevent us turning in upon ourselves. One's life has value so long as one attributes value to the life of others, by means of love, friendship, indignation, passion.[4]

She warns that men and women should not start their last years "alone and empty-handed."

To be sure, most of us are more concerned about the death of loved ones than about our own mortality. The vast majority of humankind through all ages and in all places has believed in immortality—that our lives are not lost in death but only transformed for the better. But the loss of another empties our life. Knowing that, should we predecease a loved one, we need to provide for the quality of that person's life after our passing.

A few years ago I was moved to write a book about living in the light of our mortality and immortality—*Ten Thoughts to Take into Eternity*. What I learned is particularly relevant to those of us who have reached the later part of life, namely that:

- Death doesn't hurt—life does.
- You are not the first person to make this trip.
- You *can* take it with you, every blessing in your life.
- This trip is not a vacation.
- You are not going somewhere, but to someone.
- You are not ready, but it doesn't matter.
- Be prepared for surprises.
- You are leaving nothing behind.

Living the Present Moment in the Light of Eternity

Time, Herbert Spenser noted, is something most people try to kill, adding wryly that time ends in killing them. Time is the certain messenger of mortality, ensuring that one day *everyone* will be singing "The September Song." When pubs close in England, the owner urges his customers, "Hurry up, it's time!"—an announcement to which we need be alert as we savor our remaining years. "Time goes, you say? Ah no," Robert Burns sighed. "Alas, Time stays, *we* go."[5]

Happily, there is an alternative to time and its ravages. It is eternity. The vast majority of humankind through all ages and cultures, has treasured the expectation of an afterlife. More than nine of ten Americans, young and old, express the faith that they will join all those who have ever passed through life, to reach a state where time no longer reigns.[6] Shakespeare himself insisted that time must have a stop. It ends in eternity, which—far from being an endless extension of time—is a perfect *now*.

Religion popularly regards eternity as *rest* from time and change, from regret for the past and anxiety for the future. But it is more than a mere respite; it is fulfillment. "Teach us to care, and not to care," T. S. Eliot prayed, "Teach us to sit still"—because in stillness we see. "Be still," the psalmist urged, "and know that I am God."[7]

People of faith agree that the closest experience to eternity is to live totally and gratefully in the present, undistracted by regret or nostalgia for the past, or fret for the future. In the estimation of twentieth-century French Catholic poet Paul Claudel, the richness of growing old rests in our ability to treat today as a kind of eternity within time. Strictly speaking, we have no option. The present moment is all we have, so it is worth cultivating. It is fraught with gifts, not the least of which is serenity.

Resurrection is humankind's common aspiration. We expect our spirits to rise in a new creation, unburdened of clocks and calendars. In such a timeless state, intimacy will no longer be rare and reckless, but the standard for all relationships. Pain and age will pass. Disappointment will disappear. We will survive life's struggle, and love will last.

Saint Paul conceded that, confined by time, we view reality as in a distorting mirror, but he promised that in eternity we will see clearly. Despite our lack of complete clarity, it makes sense to live the present moment in eternity's light.

Death, Where Is Thy Sting?

When Shakespeare's dour Dane, Hamlet, posed his celebrated question—"To be, or not to be?"—he gave death and life equal billing. Every healthy human instinct insists that the prince had it wrong—that life, however difficult, is infinitely preferable to oblivion. Faith and instinct alike affirm life, insisting that death is but a passage to transcendence—a brief curtain and dimming of lights before a magnificent and permanent final act.

For the faithful, death marks neither an end nor even a beginning, but a continuation and consummation of all we have loved and learned in this life. Although all humanity aspires to a life free of pain and uncertainty, few of us find it this side of eternity. But we can prepare for it now by living fully for the rest of our lives.

People who assume that survival of the *soul* is a fundamental Christian belief are gravely mistaken. In truth, the Christian creed proclaims: "I believe in the resurrection of the body, and life everlasting." The afterlife is for complete creatures who live on in a new state of unimaginable satisfaction. (No wispy, disembodied spirits in the Christian heaven!) The best preparation for the afterlife is to live fully here and now every day.

But we may be inclined to resist. As we age, our sense of mortality can become more acute and our isolation more palpable. Many of my retired friends turn first to the obituaries in the morning paper for the news that affects them most. Which of their friends and associates, they wonder, has departed this mortal oil, leaving them behind, more alone, more isolated in life as a minority of one?

Of course, everyone faces death alone and unexperienced. We are loath to leave our loved ones. And of course, we fear the pain and decline that might accompany an illness leading to death. But death itself need not be feared. Each of us has faced every major challenge in life in the same way—for the first time, with no experience, and with some trepidation. But we passed each milestone fully realizing that literally billions other men and women before us had confronted the same rites of passage and prevailed.

So with death. The vast majority of Americans have faith that it is not life's end but a new beginning that will have no end. We do not know precisely what to expect, but we know that all of humankind make the same journey. The 5.6 billion men, women, and children who share life on earth with you and me at this very moment are but a tiny minority of all who have lived before us or will be born after our departure. When you and I pass from this life, we will not be alone. We will be joining the majority.

Investing in Eternity

When the American frontier was still wild, an anonymous prospector scratched this final lament on the wall of his shack in Deadwood, South Dakota: "I lost my gun. I lost my horse. I'm out of food. The Indians are after me. But I've got all the gold I can carry."

Late in life, confronted with our own mortality, we will sense a kinship with the miner, fearing that all we have fought for and won will ultimately be stripped away, and that we must leave the gold behind.

But what if death has no dominion? Suppose that death is not a period, but merely a comma that marks a pause in our progress from this life to the next? What if the life we know is but a prelude to eternity? Then nothing we have achieved in this life can be lost but will be the gold we carry to the next.

In truth, the vast majority of humankind has always held that this life is not the end of living, and that we *can* take it with us—not fool's gold, but the wealth of affection, experience, and knowledge we have accumulated. All the more reason for living life to the full!

Given the choice between going to heaven and hearing a lecture about heaven, Oscar Wilde noted, an American would prefer the lecture. The English wit's indictment is true enough to be discomfiting. Talk is reassuring, a buffer against reality. It explains why people chatter so often and long on their cell phones.

By contrast, silence is unnerving, experience scary. We prefer impersonal adventures on the wide screen rather than true adventure in our lives. Virtual reality beats the real thing hands down. We are quick to heed the warning, "Kids, don't attempt this at home!"

Muslims are required at least once in their lifetime to leave their homes to make a pilgrimage to Mecca, presaging their ultimate journey to Paradise. It is an onerous desert journey, even for the wealthy, contrived to make the Islamic faithful take thought about the balance of their lives on earth. The afterlife will be our ultimate adventure as well, but a very foreign adventure unless we prepare now. Is our passport in order? Will we speak the language of eternity and comprehend the customs of the inhabitants? Will we recognize our host?

Our final trip will not be a vacation from life but, rather, our eternal destination. Prayer will be our passport, silence the language spoken there, love the custom of the natives in that place. Best that we prepare for the journey now while we have time.

The End of Loneliness

Even hopeful mortals are haunted by the twin enigmas of death and eternity. Both are mysteries, and it is only natural for us to shrink in the face of the unknown. But we know more about mortality and immortality than we imagine—easily enough to live confidently in the prospect of eternal life, free from the fear of death. If you are a person of faith, this knowledge can give you both hope and direction. If you are a skeptic, you will be struck nevertheless by the convergence of belief that life, once bestowed, cannot end in oblivion. Either way, you will be able to celebrate the rest of your life with greater assurance and self-worth.

Each of us, by dint of our humanity, holds the key to immortality. In truth, we cannot avoid eternity. Happily, the keys to the kingdom of heaven are sensible approaches that free our minds and spirits, not dogmas that shackle our souls.

The beginning of wisdom is to view life and death as complementary rather than adversarial. Each of us lives and dies essentially alone. No matter how many fiends and lovers we have, or how caring our families are, we are ultimately isolated in our own thoughts and emotions this side of Paradise. Our separate bodies allow us to share neither pain nor ecstasy. Metaphorically, we are separate islands in this life. But in eternity we will no longer be alone. All the more reason for making friends with our Creator before we become God's houseguest.

Begin with reverence for life, which is the foundation of faith. Gratitude is faith's motive. Upon waking each day, very young Jewish children pray gratefully: "Blessed are you, O Lord our God, King of the Universe, who removes sleep from my eyes and slumber from my eyelids. I thank you . . . for restoring my soul to me with compassion; great is your faithfulness."[8]

We neither deserve eternal life nor can win it by our effort. If heaven were only for the righteous, it would be woefully under-populated. Jesus affirmed that only God is good; the rest of us struggle to be faithful, grateful, and repentant. We are never really ready for heaven, but it doesn't matter. Heaven is God's gift to the grateful.

When you think about it (and now you will have the time to ponder), the afterlife is no more miraculous than the life we possess now. If the Creator chose to conceive the universe with all its wonders and bring you and me into existence, what would prompt God to discard what God values? Disappointment in us? Our failure to follow God's blueprint?

If there is something in ourselves to be forgiven, God is ready to do so. And if, at the end of our sojourn here, we are still not yet ready for eternity, God will prepare us to be.

Great Expectations

There are two ways to solve a problem. One is to confront it; the other, to ignore it. Even the preferred path seldom really solves the problem but merely makes it manageable. Years ago, Becky and I discovered moles tunneling around our house. By persistence we have neutralized them, but it is an uneasy truce. They will not go away. An armistice is not a victory.

We tend to regard death as a problem, ignoring its inevitability so long as we retain our vitality, and postpone confronting our mortality until the eleventh hour. Admittedly, we cannot deter death altogether, but we can conduct ourselves in a manner consistent with the benefits we expect in the next life. We will reap what we sow.

The philosopher Geddes MacGregor surmises that: "It may be that some people, after a lifetime of selfish unconcern and of talk of nothing but the stock market and football scores and sex and favorite restaurants and the latest fashion in drapes, have nothing in them capable of surviving death. Who dares say?"[9]

It is a harsh question. All the more reason to invest fully in what remains of our present lives so that we will have something in us capable not only of surviving death but anticipating our great expectations.

The Epistle of Diognetus, composed in the second century, characterized the early Christians as exiles on earth because they were citizens of heaven. The earliest Christians lived in imminent expectation of the end of life as we know it. For them, eternity had already begun. Their lives exemplified Saint Paul's conviction, "For to me, to live is Christ, and to die is gain" (Philippians 1:21).

The blind poet John Milton anticipated his demise as "the golden key that opens the palace of eternity." His countryman John Donne wrote with conviction that "I shall not live 'till I see God; and when I have seen Him, I shall never die."[10]

Our own American poet Walt Whitman exulted in the prospect of eternity:

Our life is closed, our life begins . . .

Joy, shipmate, joy!

But how can we find joy when, on passing from this life to the next, we leave everything we love behind us? The Quaker colonist William Penn replied: "They that love beyond the world cannot be separated by it. Death cannot kill what never dies, nor can spirits ever be divided that love and live in the same divine principle."[11]

Heavenly Homesickness

Evangelist Vance Havner often confided that he was homesick for heaven. The prospect of heaven infused daily significance into his life, prompting him to welcome death as the portal to eternity.

As never before, the signs of immortality surround us. In the past, history was consigned to dustbins and heroes to their graves. Today, through film and videotape, we have conferred a virtual immortality on generations of persons who have long since departed this life.

When they were very young, my daughters often pointed to the TV screen and asked, "Is that person alive?" Even adults can be permitted some confusion. On any given weekend, television brings us Marilyn Monroe, John Wayne, James Dean, and a constellation of stars whose lights will never dim. Most of the recordings I enjoy are by artists who have long since departed this life, leaving their gifts behind for us to enjoy. I have seen the Astaire-Rogers films countless times and reckon the dancing couple to be more alive than I feel at my present age. Becky and I named two of our cats Fred and Ginger to keep that couple's memory alive in our home.

Poets have long been advised by their admirers to die young so they will be remembered for their youth and vitality. By contrast, you and I will likely be remembered for how we looked and acted in the autumn of our lives. No matter. The fabric of life is all of one piece, now and hereafter. By living our remaining years in the light of eternity, we will pass from this life into the next eternally youthful and ready for adventure.

In Tibet, the bar-headed goose and gander perform an unusual ritual after mating. They rise together from the waters, wings thrust out and flapping, beaks turned straight to the sky, honking loudly. These birds enjoy a lifespan of half a century and celebrate the perpetuation of life in the same way every year. When one dies, its partner never mates again.

The peninsula across the lake from our home is too shallow for suburban developers, but friendly to Canadian geese, who find it so accommodating that they have ceased their seasonal migration and have become, in effect, U.S. citizens. They mate and raise their goslings, sojourning as families on the water. At sunrise and sunset they take to the air in precise formations, honking in high spirits, flying for no particular reason and toward no particular destination, but simply for the joy of being alive.

It is risky to assign a sense of humor to animals. But some species—like the geese—surely know joy, perhaps because they (better than we) mine the present moment of its blessings. The only way to treat life with the seriousness it deserves is with joy and a sense of our own absurdity. Unlike humans, animals live unburdened by regret for the past and anxiety about the future. Instinctively and innocently, they live in the present moment and exult in it. We do well to emulate them.

The Art of Dying

As our population ages, an extensive literature has appeared concentrating on living well in our later years, but literature aimed at helping people to die with grace has virtually disappeared. The *Ars moriendi* (The Art of Dying) in fact enjoys a long literary history extending back to the ancient Egyptian and the Tibetan Book of the Dead—detailed guidebooks to the individual's passage to the afterlife. They are echoed in the Mayan Book of the Dead in pre-Columbian America.

Among Christians, the art of dying became the subject of an extensive body of popular literature beginning in the late Middle

Ages, stimulated by the frequent plagues, famines, wars, and executions that rendered daily life uncertain and anxious. The almost palpable presence of death paralleled the decline of the church as a political and spiritual protector of the faithful. Consequently, people were thrown on their own resources to make sense of the hope given by their Savior, who long since had conquered death and promised Paradise.

The *Ars moriendi* actually taught the art of *living* in the light of certain death and cautioned against the futility of mere materialism, for, it argued, one can't carry material things into eternity. But, it added, many things can be cultivated in this life that will be possessed fully in the next, among them love, knowledge, appreciation, and even adventure. But wealth, honor, power, and lust were deemed *vanitas vanitatum* (vanity of vanities), and the faithful were urged instead to contemplate death by focusing their lives on transcendent riches encompassed in the love of God. The *Ars moriendi* aimed to assist Christians to value the present life in the light of eternity.

While skeptics may be inclined to cling futilely to their present lives for fear of the beyond, believers can make the opposite mistake of treating their present lives as trivial compared to eternity. Both assessments are faulty. This life is but the opening act to a worthy play, and death but a brief intermission. A good act establishes the plot, the pace, and the characters for the rest of the play—and so with eternity.

Betting on Eternity

Faithful or skeptical, most of us would prefer to place our bets on an afterlife rather than oblivion. But what if the prospect of Paradise is only a pipedream? What if, once asleep, we never awaken?

More than three centuries ago, the Christian philosopher Blaise Pascal attempted to answer those questions with a wager that goes like this: If you believe in God and there is indeed a God, you win eternal happiness. On the other hand, if you believe in God and he turns out to be a myth, you lose nothing. But if you reject faith in God, and God does exist, then you lose everything for all eternity. Pascal's conclusion: the only losers in life are those who reject God.

Gambling on God has never attracted me. It assumes that the object of faith is to cash in on an eternal payoff. Moreover, Pascal's wager suggests that God punishes people who, for whatever reason, lack faith. That will not do either. But give the philosopher his due. He was writing at a time when faithful living involved great sacrifices, and when those who turned from religion did so to pursue lives of sensuality and corruption. With his wager, Pascal was simply reassuring people who believed in God that it was a good bet to follow God's will. Pascal didn't address the virtuous person who, for whatever reason, didn't share his religious faith.

Let's take the worst-case scenario. Suppose that when our lives end, that's all there is. First off, we won't realize the loss because there will no longer be a "we" to experience it. Alone, that wouldn't justify our having lived lives of self-deception. But look at it this way: integrity and love are their own rewards. It is sane to be faithful and compassionate, and gratifying to be grateful. Everyone who truly relishes life will revere it and be responsible to it, whatever his or her faith.

As I enter the final seasons of my life, I hope not to lose Pascal's wager, but my religious faith is not just a bet on an afterlife. Rather, I am betting on a God who sent his Son to live this life with us, to die for us, and to transform himself and us in the process. That is no pipedream.

If you and I do not share the same faith, we still share the same Creator, the same aspirations, and the same destiny. There is no onus to being a reluctant believer or searching skeptic. It is sensible to be skeptical and to shrink from something as complicated as faith and from someone as demanding as God. Nevertheless, there is wisdom in the saying that unless we stand for something, we will fall for anything.

The epistle to the Hebrews states that "faith is being sure of what we hope for and certain of what we do not see" (11:1). In other words, faith gives substance to our hope and vision to our love. And love is eternal.

The fear of every person who struggles with faith, hope, and doubt is well founded, and I share it with you. But to know God is to love God, and love conquers timidity. Grace abounds and, if we let it, will transform us into new creatures suited for new life. The proper attitude toward life is gratitude and humor. As you anticipate your later years, begin extracting the most from each moment, living it in the light of eternity. Stanford University researchers report that most of the truly traumatic incidents in people's lives take place before we reach the age of twenty-six. By contrast, older people are more likely to be serene, savoring life, fearless of death.

Laid to Rest

The acerbic author Evelyn Waugh famously ridiculed the funeral industry in his novel, *The Loved One*. When Jessica Mitford followed up with *The American Way of Death*, a non-fictional exposé of those who profit commercially from bereavement, Waugh complained that "the trouble with Miss Mitford is that she has no stated attitude towards death." The lady retorted, "I *do* have an attitude towards death. I'm against it."[12] But death happens, and it does not hurt the deceased. Rather, it is the survivors who are bereaved.

In the garden of the Yount home we have what amounts to a pet cemetery. At the moment it is the final resting place for four cats and two dogs. Each has a small metal plate for a marker, with the pet's name and years noted, plus a sentiment. For Bess, our first Scottish terrier, it reads, "She blessed our lives." For her successor, Fiona: "Our best friend." For the cats: "Braveheart," "Mr. First Nighter," "Remember me," and "Matchless spirit." Assorted wounded birds, squirrels, and rabbits, which Becky and I tried unsuccessfully to nurse back to health, are also there in unmarked graves.

The sorrow one feels on the passing of a pet is surpassed by the grief survivors endure when a human loved one passes from their lives. The American funeral industry exists because we cannot face burying one of our own, and aren't allowed to in any case. Instead some twenty-one thousand funeral homes in the United States handle two million deaths every year.

Unlike other industries, which aim by advertising to increase demand for their products and services, the funeral industry is in no position to encourage more people to die. As a result, the business of dying is burdened by over-capacity and under-utilization. Many funeral homes handle as few as one funeral a week. The only way they can survive is to charge exorbitant fees, playing on the guilt and grief of survivors.

In his best-selling classic, *Dealing Creatively with Death*, Ernest Morgan notes that "most bereaved relatives, in a state of shock and grief following a death, see no alternative to accepting what a funeral director presents as proper and acceptable."[13] Ironically, funeral costs in recent years have risen at double the rate of the cost of *living*. Even a decade ago the average cost of dying was $6,000. Today it is over $10,000.

In an effort to cut costs and spare their survivors the ordeal of making arrangements, some people choose to prepay for funeral services and cemetery plot. My parents did, and funeral directors are delighted to collect in advance. But the savings, if any, are slight, and many people nowadays are uncertain where they will reside when they die. Better to join the nearest memorial society, which surveys and compares funeral and internment charges in your area. Dues for our local society are just $5 a year. If you can't find a local phone listing, send a dollar to the Continental Association of Funeral and Memorial Societies, 6900 Lost Lake Road, Egg Harbor, WI 57209, and ask for an up-to-date list across the United States and Canada. Or check the AARP Web site: http://www.aarp.org/confacts/money/funeral/html.

Rock-bottom costs can be as low as $725 for direct cremation, $600 for immediate burial, and $1,700 for a standard funeral. Urns can cost as little as $25, caskets $395. On application, Social Security provides $255 toward final costs; the Veterans Administration pays more. Most religious faiths approve of cremation, and one in five Americans now choose it over burial. Incidentally, you don't have to purchase an urn from a funeral director but can provide your own container.

"I'll Do It My Way."

The people who leapt from the collapsing World Trade Towers did not choose death, but only a quicker, less painful way than being crushed or burned. By contrast, there is a growing movement to choose the time, place, and method of dying, preferably with the assistance of a physician. Dr. Kevorkian was not the only advocate for euthanasia, just the most vocal.

Many physicians will admit privately that they have, on occasion, either overmedicated the terminally ill or withheld life-extending treatment for those in a coma or in pain. The effect is to hasten death but not to "pull the plug" on a patient's life. The purpose of a living will is to inform your doctor that you do not want to be kept alive artificially in a terminal illness. Death in any event tends to come quickly to those who lose the will to live.

Euthanasia is something else altogether. It is asking to die or killing oneself—suicide. In 1990 alone, Derek Humphrey's book, *Final Exit*, topped the *New York Times* best-seller list and sold half a million copies. It is an explicit guide to taking one's own life with minimal pain and trouble. But some terminally ill persons are physically unable to follow Humphrey's instructions, hence the demand for physician assistance.

Suicide is most prevalent among young Americans, not the elderly. Nevertheless, AARP reveals that white males sixty-five and older have the highest suicide rate, four times the national average, far outstripping the suicide rate for older women. Clinical depression, which can be treated, is seldom the cause, nor is terminal illness, physical disability, or chronic pain. Rather, it's loss of spouse, friends, health, and a meaningful role in society, says the AARP report. "More older people are committing suicide . . . because they just don't want to go on living. They are projecting what's ahead, and just don't want to go through with it."[14]

Betty Friedan believes the "right to die" movement "may pave the way or serve the interests of powerful forces who need scapegoats to divert people's attention from desperately needed reforms in our economy and our educational and health care systems." Older people are reluctant to be a burden on others and an expense to loved ones even when they have years left to live in tolerable health. "An awful lot of suicide in old age doesn't get reported as suicide," says Dr. Robert Butler. AARP notes that older people who choose to die are more likely than younger persons to succeed: "The elderly can more easily commit 'covert suicide' by starving themselves, terminating life-sustaining medications or overdosing on prescribed medications. Such suicides may also be disguised as fatal accidents."[15]

Religion condemns suicide because it reveres life and worships the Creator who gives life. Faith acknowledges that ultimately we do not belong to ourselves but to God. British neurologist Ann

Coxon treats patients who, like physicist Stephen Hawking, are seriously disabled, yet maintain a zest for living. "You mean I'm going to be a beached whale?" a patient with progressive paralysis asked Dr. Coxon. "Yes," she answered, "but as your body gets weaker, your mind will soar, and you will be able to communicate that to your children in a way that will be a great gift to them."[16]

Letting Go

Anticipating his death at the age of ninety-four, George Bernard Shaw joked, "I knew that if I hung around here long enough, something like this was bound to happen." His advice to his survivors: "Do not try to live forever. You will not succeed." Oscar Wilde, breathing his last in a cheap Paris hotel room, addressed its hideous wallpaper with the challenge: "One of us has got to go!"[17]

Elisabeth Kübler-Ross remarks of people informed of terminal illness that they go through five stages, starting with denial, then anger, then bargaining with God. When that gambit fails, they fall into depression, which at length is dissipated by acceptance.[18]

Oddly, she makes no mention of humor or liberation at the end. But, in fact, most people who have lived full lives are utterly reconciled to death and meet it with lightheartedness as liberation from all that has limited them this side of eternity, not least the burdens of aging. Death doesn't hurt, they know, but life often does and has. The millions of men, women, and children who have undergone "near-death" experience report it as euphoric and ecstatic. The *causes* of death are sometimes painful, of course, but physicians who tend regularly to the dying report death itself to be peaceful.

Nobel Peace Prize winner Albert Schweitzer advises us "not to close our eyes" to the inevitable: "Let us pause for a moment, look at the distant view, and then carry on. Thinking about death in this way produces love for life. When we are familiar with death, we accept each week, each day, as a gift. Only if we are able thus to accept life—bit by bit—does it become precious."[19]

Where wakes and funerals were once standard, memorial services are now common. In one sense they insulate mourners from death, treating the loved one as but a memory. Still, in my own recent experience, memorial services have been occasions for celebrating the life of the deceased, often with lighthearted anecdotes, and always with love and respect. Such remembrances are life-affirming and filled with hope, especially for survivors. I hope that people whom I cherish will find something to chuckle about when they look back on my life.

Curse or Blessing?

Psychiatrist Scott Peck tells the story of being consulted by four aging women who came to him with the same complaint: depression at growing old. He said, "Each was secular-minded. Each had either made money or married money. All their children had turned out golden. It was as if life had gone according to a script. But now they were getting cataracts, requiring hearing aids or dentures, and facing hip replacements. This wasn't the way they would have written the script, and they were angry and depressed. I saw no way to help them without converting them to a vision of old age as something more than a meaningless time of watching themselves simply rot away. I tried to help them 'buy it' as a spiritual period in their lives, a time of preparation."

It was, Dr. Peck confesses, not an easy sell. His message— "Look, you're not the scriptwriter; it's just not entirely your show"—fell on deaf ears.

He was more successful with a woman in her sixties whose fierce independence was tempered by religious faith. Practically blind, she was now dependent on others. Peck counseled her: "You've been a very successful person, and I think you needed that pride for your many accomplishments. But you know, it's a journey from here to heaven, and it's a good rule of journeying to travel light. I'm not sure how successful you're going to be in getting to heaven, carrying around all this pride. You see your blindness as a curse, and I don't blame you. Conceivably, however, you might look at it as a blessing designed to relieve you of the no longer necessary burden of your pride. Except for your eyes, you're in pretty good health. You've probably got at least a dozen more years to live. It's up to you whether you'd rather live those years with a curse or a blessing."

By rights, the later years of one's life ought to be rich in appreciation and serenity. But it is also a time for preparation for the life beyond this life. In Dr. Peck's words, it "includes the fearsome learning of how to consciously give up control of our lives when it is appropriate to do so—and ultimately hand ourselves over to God."[20]

Go Gentle into That Good Night

The acerbic novelist Gore Vidal has long since designated a place to be laid to rest in Washington's Rock Creek Cemetery. When, in the autumn of his life, Vidal was asked what he wished to have inscribed on his tombstone, he readily replied:

"To Be Continued"

That is precisely what every person of faith defines death to be—a mere intermission between life and eternity—something worth preparing for when we reach September. There will be no cause to rage against the dying of the light. We will go gentle into that good night—to an eternal dawn.

Acknowledgments

I launched this small book with these lines from William Blake:

To see a World in a Grain of Sand
And a Heaven in a Wild Flower
Hold Infinity in the palm of your hand
And Eternity in an Hour.

I believe these aspirations are not only appropriate to the next stage of our lives but achievable this side of paradise. While you and I must keep active as we age, we also need to be meditative and appreciative. There is time now for long thoughts and even longer loves. All we need is the inclination to ponder and to care.

As our physical eyesight falters, our spiritual insight can grow. If we will but take the time, we can see a world in a grain of sand and a heaven in a wild flower. God has always held the whole world in God's hand. If we will but extend our own hands, we can touch the border of infinity. If we will live fully in the present moment—without regret for the past or anxiety for the future— we can contain eternity in an hour.

My agent, Deborah Grosvenor, supported this project before I set a word on paper and had only a working title rattling around in my head. "It sounds like the sort of book I could give my mother," she said. High praise! I am grateful that Deborah keeps championing my work.

My thanks, too, to editors Lois Wallentine, Rochelle Melander, and Michelle L. N. Cook for shepherding the manuscript into print, to Laurie Ingram for the delightful cover design, and to Carol Van Dyke for promoting it.

As ever, my wife, Becky, was my masterful muse and critic, and I dedicate the book to her, borrowing Browning's brave lines: "Grow old along with me. The best is yet to be."

In the course of writing, I leaned on some three dozen other authors for their wisdom about aging with grace, most heavily on B. F. Skinner and John Mortimer, whose books I recommend. My thanks to them all. I also borrowed briefly from three of my own recent books, unable to state better now what I wrote then.

My constant companion during composition was Henry David Thoreau. I first read *Walden* as a youth. Back then it woke me to the wonder of life and living. I find it even more evocative and practical now. During the course of writing the book you hold, *Walden* became my bedtime reading, reawakening me to the perennial wisdom that "only that day dawns to which we are awake."

David Yount
Montclair, Virginia

Notes

Preface

1. Quoted by Michael Dirda, "Readings," *Washington Post Book World*, April 22, 2001, 15.
2. Chris Warren, "Separate But Equal," *Fidelity*, May 2004, 9.
3. *The World Almanac and Book of Facts* (New York: World Almanac Books, 2004), 14.
4. Ibid.
5. Anecdote related by George Carey, Archbishop of Canterbury, at the College of Preachers, Washington, D.C., October 6, 2002.
6. *World Almanac*, 13.
7. David Yount, *Ten Thoughts to Take into Eternity* (New York: Simon & Schuster, 1999).
8. Albert B. Cranshaw, "A Lost Retirement Dream for Boomers?" *Washington Post*, December 7, 2003, F4.
9. Lord Byron, Journals, quoted in John Bartlett, *Familiar Quotations,* 15th ed. (Boston: Little, Brown, 1980), 458.
10. Quoted by John Mortimer, *The Summer of a Dormouse* (New York: Viking, 2002), 5.
11. Cranshaw, "A Lost Retirement," F4.
12. Quoted by Hugh Downs, *Fifty to Forever* (Nashville: Thomas Nelson, 1994), 13ff.
13. Jimmy Carter, *The Virtues of Aging* (New York: Ballantine, 1998), 15.
14. George Gallup, Jr., Gallup Tuesday Briefing, 2002.
15. Chalmer M. Roberts, *How Did I Get Here So Fast?* (New York: Warner Books, 1991), 33.
16. George Eliot, *Adam Bede,* quoted in Bartlett, *Familiar Quotations,* 564.
17. Oscar Wilde, *De Profundis,* quoted in Bartlett, *Familiar Quotations,* 676.

1. From This Day Forward

1. Aldous Huxley, *Collected Essays* (London: Chatto and Windus, 1960), viii.
2. B. F. Skinner and M. E. Vaughan, *Enjoy Old Age: A Practical Guide* (New York: W. W. Norton, 1983 and 1997), 9-10.
3. *World Almanac*, 268.
4. Horace Deets, "My Word," *Modern Maturity*, May-June, 2001, 13.
5. Ibid.
6. Ibid.
7. *World Almanac*, 143.
8. John Langone, *Growing Older* (Boston: Little, Brown, 1991), 3.
9. Quoted by Michael Dirda, "Readings," 15.
10. Richard Morin, "Unhealthy Paradox," *Washington Post*, May 20, 2001, B5.
11. Simone de Beauvoir, *The Coming of Age* (New York: Putnam's, 1972), 13.
12. Downs, *Fifty to Forever*, 7-8.
13. Ibid.
14. Ibid., 9
15. Thomas Moore, *The Re-Enchantment of Everyday Life* (New York: HarperCollins, 1996), 75.
16. Quoted by George Will, "Honoring John Adams and Family," *Washington Post*, September 17, 2001, A26.
17. Quoted by Skinner, *Enjoy Old Age*, 105.
18. See David Yount, *Spiritual Simplicity* (New York: Simon & Schuster, 1997).

19. Quoted by de Beauvoir, *The Coming of Age*, 1.
20. Percy Bysshe Shelley, "Adonais," in *The Complete Works* (London: Oxford University Press, 1961), 443.
21. Obituary, *Washington Post*, June 30, 2001, B7.
22. Cherry Norton, "Secrets of the Isle of Eternal Youth," *Sunday Times* (London), June 10, 2001, 4-12.
23. Ibid.
24. Ibid.
25. Tamara K. Hareven, "The Last Stage: Historical Adulthood and Old Age," in *Adulthood*, ed. Erik Erickson 201ff. (New York: W.W. Norton, 1978).
26. Ibid.
27. Ibid., 15.
28. Bartlett, *Familiar Quotations,* 835.
29. Graham Greene, *A Sort of Life* (New York: Pocket Books, 1978), 13.

2. Forsaking All Others

1. Henry David Thoreau, *Walden* (Philadelphia: Courage Books, 1987).
2. Ibid., 18.
3. Ibid., 10.
4. Ibid., 9.
5. Ibid., 12.
6. Dirda, "Readings," 15.
7. Ibid.
8. Ibid.
9. Thoreau, *Walden*, 90.
10. Creighton University report, 2001.
11. David Yount, *Faith Under Fire* (Pittsburgh: SterlingHouse, 2004), 74.
12. Yount, *Spiritual Simplicity*, 76-77.
13. Morin, "Unhealthy Paradox," B5.
14. Skinner, *Enjoy Old Age*, 133.
15. Ibid., 135.
16. Alan Wolfe, *Moral Freedom* (New York: W. W. Norton, 2001), 1.
17. Skinner, *Enjoy Old Age*, 135.
18. Ibid., 139.
19. M. Scott Peck, *The Road Less Traveled and Beyond* (New York: Simon & Schuster, 1997), 137.

3. For Better, for Worse

1. Victoria Price, *Vincent Price: A Daughter's Biography* (New York: St. Martin's Press, 1999), 430.
2. Ibid., 448.
3. Ibid.
4. Louis Menand, "Laura's World," *New Yorker*, July 2, 2001, 81-84.
5. Skinner, *Enjoy Old Age*, 117.
6. *Modern Maturity*, July-August 2001, 26.
7. Morin, "Unhealthy Paradox," B5.
8. Ibid.
9. Ruth Gledhill, "Vicars Prove Forgetful," *Sunday Times* (London), November 25, 2001, A1.
10. Roberts, *How Did I Get Here So Fast?*, 53.

4. For Richer, for Poorer

1. Stan Hinden, "Is There Enough for a Nest?" *Washington Post*, August 26, 2001, H1-H4.
2. Ibid.
3. Ibid.
4. Andrew Tobias, *The Only Investment Guide You'll Ever Need* (New York: Harcourt, 1991), 68.
5. Morin, "Unhealthy Paradox," B5.
6. Andrew M. Greeley, *Faithful Attraction* (New York: TOR) 170ff.
7. Morin, "Unhealthy Paradox," B5.
8. Thomas Moore, *The Re-Enchantment of Everyday Life* (New York: HarperCollins, 1996), 15.
9. Michelle Singletary, "Financial Planning Crucial for People with Special Needs," *Washington Post,* August 26, 2001, H1-H4.
10. Ibid.
11. Lionel Tiger, *The Pursuit of Pleasure* (Boston: Little, Brown, 1992), 13.
12. Ibid.
13. David Yount, *Second Chances* (unpublished manuscript), 132.

5. In Sickness and in Health

1. Bartlett, *Familiar Quotations*, 851.
2. Phillip Longman, "The Limits of Medicine," *Washington Post,* March 31, 2004, A25.
3. Ibid.
4. Ibid.
5. Ibid.
6. Ibid.
7. Ibid.
8. Ibid.
9. Ibid.
10. Ibid.
11. Ibid.
12. Ibid.
13. David Yount, *Till Death Do Us Part* (unpublished manuscript), 111.
14. Greg Anderson, *22 Laws of Wellness* (San Francisco: HarperSanFrancisco, 1996), 3-4.
15. C. S. Lewis, *The Problem of Pain* (New York: Macmillan, 1962), 89.
16. Ibid.
17. Bernie Siegel, *Love, Medicine, and Miracles* (New York: Harper & Row, 1986), 15.
18. Franz Alexander, *Fundamentals of Psychoanalysis* (New York: W. W. Norton, 1963), 5.
19. John Robert McFarland, *Now That I Have Cancer* (Kansas City: Andrews and McMeel, 1993), 113.
20. D. Keith Mano, *The Bridge* (New York: Doubleday, 1973), 95.
21. Longman, "Limits of Medicine," A25.
22. Siegel, *Love, Medicine, and Miracles*, 210-11.
23. Ibid., 195.
24. Ibid.
25. Longman, "Limits of Medicine," A25
26. Ibid.
27. John Knowles, *Peace Breaks Out* (New York: Holt, Rinehart & Winston, 1981), 5.
28. Siegel, *Love, Medicine, and Miracles*, 113.
29. Ibid., 15

30. Ibid.
31. Ibid.
32. Bartlett, *Familiar Quotations*, 650.
33. Ben Stein, "Slippery When 'Vette," *Modern Maturity,* July-August 2001, 32-36.

6. To Love and to Cherish
1. Quoted in Bartlett, *Familiar Quotations,* 697.
2. *World Almanac*, 14.
3. Andrew M. Greeley, *Faithful Attraction* (New York: Tor, 1992), 193.
4. Bartlett, *Familiar Quotations*, 678.
5. Elizabeth Enright, *AARP Magazine*, July-August 2004, 56-59.
6. Greeley, *Faithful Attraction*, 34-35.
7. Chalmer M. Roberts, "The View from 90," *Washington Post*, January 23, 2001, H15-H16.
8. Barbara De Angelis, *Ask Barbara: The 100 Most Asked Questions about Love, Sex, and Relationships* (New York: Dell, 1998), 95.
9. Greeley, *Faithful Attraction*, 106 ff.
10. Michele Nicolosi, "Never Too Old," *Washington Post*, July 17, 2001, 10-12.
11. Robin Fields, "A Late Change in Lifestyle," *Washington Post*, August 31, 2001, C3.
12. Lionel Tiger, *The Pursuit of Pleasure* (Boston: Little, Brown, 1992), 3.
13. David G. Myers, *The Pursuit of Happiness* (New York: Morrow, 1992), 211.
14. William Shatner, *Get a Life* (New York: Pocket Books, 1999), 13.
15. Peter Mayle, *Acquired Tastes* (New York: Bantam Books, 1992), 15.
16. *Times* (London), "News Review," October 1, 1921.
17. Robert Bellah et al., *Habits of the Heart* (Berkeley: University of California Press, 1996), 11ff.
18. Robert D. Putnam, *Bowling Alone: The Collapse and Revival of American Community* (New York: Simon and Schuster, 2000), 15-28.
19. Tiger, *Pursuit of Pleasure*, 215.
20. John Punshon, *Portrait in Grey* (London: Quaker Home Service), 101.

7. To Have and to Hold
1. Bergen Evans, ed., *Dictionary of Quotations* (New York: Wings Books, 1969), 411.
2. Mortimer, *The Summer of a Dormouse,* 1.
3. Ibid.
4. Ibid., 45.
5. Morgan, *Dealing Creatively with Death*, 14.
6. Stephanie Strom, "Charitable Giving Holds Steady, Report Finds," *New York Times*, June 22, 2004, 13.
7. William Shakespeare, *Hamlet*, quoted in Bartlett, *Familiar Quotations,* 221.
8. G. K. Chesterton, "St. Francis of Assisi," in *Collected Works* (San Francisco: Ignatius Press, 1986), 30.
9. Thoreau, *Walden*, 190.
10. Ibid.
11. Ibid.
12. Ibid., 193.
13. Ibid., 192.
14. Ibid., 196.

8. Till Death Do Us Part

1. "September 11, 2001," *New Yorker*, September 24, 2001, 71-2.
2. Bartlett, *Familiar Quotations*, 456.
3. de Beauvoir, *Coming of Age*, 5-6.
4. Ibid.
5. David Yount, *Breaking through God's Silence* (New York: Simon & Schuster, 1996), 75-80.
6. Ibid.
7. Ibid.
8. S. Singer, *Authorized Daily Prayer Book of the United Hebrew Congregations of the Commonwealth* (Cambridge, Mass.: Press Syndicate, n.d.), 830.
9. Mary Batchelor, *The Lion Prayer Collection* (Oxford: Lion), 18.
10. David Yount, *Ten Thoughts to Take into Eternity* (New York: Simon & Schuster, 1999), 9.
11. Bartlett, *Familiar Quotations*, 314.
12. Yount, *Ten Thoughts*, 39.
13. Ernest Morgan, *Dealing Creatively with Death* (Bayside, N.J.: Zinn Communications, 1994), 14.
14. "Hard Questions," *Modern Maturity*, July-August 2001, 26-28.
15. Ibid.
16. Siegel, *Love, Medicine, and Miracles.* 74.
17. Jonathon Green, ed., *Famous Last Words* (London: Kyle Cathie Ltd., 1997), 87.
18. Elisabeth Kübler-Ross, *Questions and Answers on Death and Dying* (New York: Scribner, 1993).
19. Bartlett, *Familiar Quotations*, 756.
20. Peck, *The Road Less Traveled*, 173-175.

Bibliography

Anderson, Hugh. "The Book of Job," in Charles M. Laymon, *The Interpreter's One-Volume Commentary on the Bible.* Nashville: Abingdon, 1971.

Carter, Jimmy. *Living Faith.* New York: Times Books, 1996.

————. *The Virtues of Aging.* New York: Ballantine, 1998.

Claffin, Edward, ed. *Age Protectors.* New York: Rodale, 1998.

De Angelis, Barbara. *The Real Rules.* New York: Dell, 1997.

de Beauvoir, Simone. *The Coming of Age.* New York: Putnam, 1972.

Downs, Hugh. *Fifty to Forever.* Nashville: Thomas Nelson, 1994.

Erickson, Erik H., ed. *Adulthood.* New York: Norton, 1978.

Friedan, Betty. *The Fountain of Age.* New York: Simon & Schuster, 1993.

Goldman, Connie, and Richard Mahler. *Secrets of Becoming a Late Bloomer.* Center City, Minn.: Hazelden, 1995.

Greeley, Andrew M. *Faithful Attraction.* New York: Tor, 1992.

Green, Jonathon, ed. *Famous Last Words.* London: Kyle Cathie Ltd., 1979.

Harding, Rachel, and Mary Dyson. *A Book of Condolences*. New York: Continuum, 1981.

Kidder, Tracy. *Old Friends*. Boston: Houghton Mifflin, 1993.

Langone, John. *Growing Older*. Boston: Little, Brown, 1991.

Lewis, C. S. *The Four Loves*. New York: Harcourt, Brace, 1960.

———. *God in the Dock*. Grand Rapids, Mich.: Eerdmans, 1970.

———. *The Problem of Pain*. New York: Macmillan, 1962.

Medina, John J. *The Clock of Ages*. Cambridge: Cambridge University Press, 1996.

Metzger, Bruce M., and Michael D. Coogan. *The Oxford Companion to the Bible*. New York: Oxford University Press, 1993.

Moore, Thomas. *Care of the Soul*. New York: HarperCollins, 1992.

———. *The Re-Enchantment of Everyday Life*. New York: HarperCollins, 1996.

———. *The Soul of Sex*. New York: HarperCollins, 1998.

Mortimer, John. *The Summer of a Dormouse*. New York: Viking, 2000.

Myers, David G. *The Pursuit of Happiness*. New York: Morrow, 1992.

Peck, M. Scott. *Further Along the Road Less Traveled*. New York: Simon & Schuster, 1993.

———. *The Road Less Traveled and Beyond*. New York: Simon & Schuster, 1997.

Peterson, Peter G. *Gray Dawn*. New York: Times Books, 1999.

Pogrebin, Letti Cottin. *Getting Over Getting Older*. Boston: Little, Brown, 1996.

Price, Victoria. *Vincent Price: A Daughter's Biography*. New York: St. Martin's Press, 1999.

Putnam, Robert D. *Bowling Alone: The Collapse and Revival of American Community*. New York: Simon & Schuster, 2000.

Roberts, Chalmer M. *How Did I Get Here So Fast?* New York: Warner Books, 1991.

Schrader, Constance. *1001 Things Everyone Over 55 Should Know*. New York: Doubleday, 1999.

Siegel, MD, Bernie S. *Love, Medicine, and Miracles*. New York: Harper & Row, 1986.

Skinner, B. F., and M. E. Vaughan. *Enjoy Old Age: A Practical Guide*. New York: Norton, 1997.

Steinem, Gloria. *Revolution From Within: A Book of Self-Esteem*. Boston: Little, Brown, 1992.

Storr, Anthony. *The Integrity of the Personality*. New York: Ballantine, l992.

Theroux, Phyllis, ed. *The Book of Eulogies*. New York: Scribner, 1997.

Thoreau, Henry David. *Walden*. New Haven, Conn.: Yale University Press, 2004.

Tiger, Lionel. *The Pursuit of Pleasure*. Boston: Little, Brown, 1992.

Wolfe, Alan. *Moral Freedom*. New York: Norton, 2001.

———. *One Nation, After All*. New York: Viking Penguin, 1998.

Yount, David. *Be Strong and Courageous*. Lanham, Md.: Sheed & Ward, 2000.

———. *Spiritual Simplicity*. New York: Simon & Schuster, 1997.

———. *Ten Thoughts to Take into Eternity*. New York: Simon & Schuster, 1999.

Books by David Yount

Growing in Faith: A Guide for the Reluctant Christian

Breaking through God's Silence: A Guide to Effective Prayer

Spiritual Simplicity: Simplify Your Life and Refresh Your Soul

Ten Thoughts to Take into Eternity: Living Wisely in the Light of the Afterlife

Be Strong and Courageous: Letters to My Children about Being Christian

What Are We to Do?: Living the Sermon on the Mount

Faith Under Fire: Religion's Role in the American Dream

The Future of Christian Faith in America

Celebrating the Rest of Your Life: A Baby Boomer's Guide to Spirituality

Visit David Yount on the Internet: http://www.erols.com/dyount
He answers reader mail at P.O. Box 2758, Woodbridge, VA 22193
and dyount@erols.com.

Dr. Yount maintains a limited speaking schedule on the subjects
of his books and columns and leads retreats and quiet days. If
your local newspaper does not carry his Scripps Howard column,
"Amazing Grace," ask your editor to consider it.